Flipping
the Script

"Diversity matters, inclusion matters, and representation matters, but too often we're afraid to be the one to speak up for what we know is right. In *Flipping the Script*, AJ's voice and message of hope comes through loud and clear!"

—Van Jones, *New York Times* bestselling author, host of *The Van Jones Show* on CNN

"The perfect book for anyone who has struggled to pick themselves up after the going gets tough. AJ's funny, insightful, relatable stories in *Flipping the Script* will make you believe that no low is too low to rewrite your life story!"

—Natalie Morales, *The Today Show, Access Live, Access*, and author of At *Home with Natalie*

"*Flipping the Script* is a great read for anyone who's ever experienced the trauma of loss, heartache, judgment, or failure. The lies we tell ourselves can be so damaging, but AJ's stories offer hope and act as a reminder that we are always just one choice away from turning our lives around!"

—Dr. Mike Dow, New York Times bestselling author of *Chicken Soup for the Soul: Think, Act & Be Happy*

"*Flipping the Script* is a MUST read! The world is a place where everybody is somebody, and nobody should be a stranger. The world is your community; go out and embrace it. LIVE LOVE LAUGH!"

—Vivica A Fox, actress, producer, entrepreneur, bestselling author of *Every Day I'm Hustling*

"I remember when AJ and I were talking, and he started to tell me a little bit about his story. I was completely in awe of him. Then, he told me he was writing a book, and I was super excited because I really felt people would benefit from hearing not only his story, but his beautiful and honest way of looking at life. I am so proud of him and so excited for people to read this book. I literally couldn't put it down!"

—Laura Marano, actress, singer

"AJ is a great guy with a huge heart! We need more voices like his out there right now and *Flipping the Script* will help give people the courage to use their own voices, regardless of their background or current situation. Communication is the way forward and this book is a great step in the right direction!"

—Jay Ellis, actor

"Amazing things happen when you realize your worth and find the courage to chase your dreams! AJ's personal stories in *Flipping the Script* are funny, yet poignant in a way that will light a fire in your heart and remind you to keep fighting for YOUR version of happiness!"

—Lisa Rinna, actress, host, entrepreneur, *New York Times* bestselling author of *Rinnavation*

"When the going gets tough, my friend AJ shows us that any script—no matter how messed up and depressing it may seem—can be written into a powerful, inspiring story! If you're up against a lot of obstacles in your life… GET THIS BOOK!"

—Sway Calloway, host of *TRL* on MTV & *Sway in the Morning* on SiriusXM

"In life, we all face our share of 'rock bottom' moments, but in *Flipping the Script* we are reminded that how we rise is far more powerful than how often we fall. This book is perfect for anyone who has ever had to fight for happiness against all odds."

—Rachel Platten, Platinum & Emmy Winning, singer/songwriter

"Authenticity is more important now than ever. *Flipping the Script* is an authentic look at the life of a young man who grew up in a conservative town, moved to a liberal city, and has a deep love for both! We're all in this thing called life together and AJ's story is a great reminder of our shared humanity!"

—SE Cupp, CNN Commentator, *New York Daily News* columnist, host of *SE Cupp Unfiltered* on HLN

"If you are going through a difficult season in your life—such as a job loss, an impossible situation, or a struggle with your own identity—AJ's stories in *Flipping the Script* will inspire you to believe that if he can achieve his dreams, then you can too!"

—Dr. Therese Mascardo, PsyD, Licensed Clinical Psychologist, founder of Exploring Therapy

"AJ has been a friend of mine since we were teenagers, and I am so proud of the compassionate man he has become. *Flipping the Script* would have benefited us both as young boys growing up in rural Ohio and struggling through our own '*rock bottom*' moments while navigating towards our authentic selves. I can't wait to see how many lives this book will positively impact!"

—Jonathan Bennett, TV Host, actor, *Mean Girls*

"I've known AJ for a few years now and I can't wait for the world to know his story! Life can be crazy, but *Flipping the Script* is a great reminder that anything is possible if you're willing to put in the work and take a leap of faith!"

—Jessie James Decker, Country Pop singer/songwriter, TV personality & fashion mogul

"*Flipping the Script* speaks to the power of the human spirit to overcome obstacles and fight for the life you deserve! AJ's story is heartbreaking at times, hilarious at others, and relatable throughout! This book is a great read for anyone who needs to be reminded that their story matters and that they are worth it!"

—Yvette Nicole Brown, actress, host, comedian, and "Champion of Kindness"

"*Flipping the Script* is a MUST READ for anyone determined to make something of themselves in the midst of hopelessness and despair, the discouragement of others, and impossible odds!"

—Amber Riley, actress, singer

"AJ lived what everyone in Hollywood knows, but no one wants to believe; we are ALL REPLACEABLE! This book is a truthful look at just how heartbreaking and challenging chasing your dream can be. Bravo AJ!"

—Keltie Knight, Emmy winner, Entertainment Tonight, co-creator of *The Lady Gang* podcast

"It's so important that strong voices from the LGBTQ community are heard and in *Flipping the Script*, AJ's voice comes through loud and clear! This book is heartfelt, heartbreaking, and hopeful all at the same time! Such a great read!"

—Kingsley, comedian & LGBTQ advocate

"Lots of people hit rock bottom—sometimes more than once. *Flipping the Script* reminds us that how we rise is more important than how we fell down. This book is for anyone who has ever worked hard to find happiness."

—Soledad O'Brien, Emmy Winning broadcast journalist, executive producer & entrepreneur, host of *Matter of Fact with Soledad O'Brien*

"AJ is the most AUTHENTIC public figure in main stream media today. His ability to share his truth is transforming the way that we relate to celebrity culture and the human experience! His real life stories will leave you thinking, 'Oh my God, I went through that too!' in the most refreshing and personal way."

—Erika De La Cruz, TV host, bestselling author & founder of Passion to Paycheck

"When you first meet AJ, you'll immediately be drawn to his personality, charm, and charisma. By reading *Flipping the Script*, you'll get to know who he is as a person. His work ethic, passion for what he does, and determination to never give up on what he believes in is so motivating. AJ's story will surely inspire you!"

—Lindsay Ell, Country music artist

"I first met AJ on the set of *Expedition Impossible* back in 2011 where I learned a lot about who he is in the face of challenges. I know his heart and it comes through crystal clear on every page of *Flipping the Script*! We've all got a story and AJ shares his in a compelling way."

—Akbar Gbajabiamila, host of *American Ninja Warrior* & NFL Network's
Fantasy Live

"No matter what your professional or personal path is or will be, adversity is going to be part of the equation. It's our job to add patience and persistence into that equation, and AJ has shed light on how important that is in *Flipping the Script*—fantastic and inspiring!"

—Dustin Lynch, Country music artist

"If you're standing at the open window of your life, wondering what you have to live for, THIS is the book that will remind you why you matter. AJ Gibson is a real, raw, uplifting human being who has been there and done that—and is ready to help others get where they want to go. You don't have to fit any specific demographic, background, or belief system to learn something big from AJ's story. Stop reading this review and start reading the book!"

—Melanie Spring, Approachable Badass & Brand Strategist, creator of
SPEAK with Confidence

Flipping the Script

Bouncing Back From Life's Rock Bottom Moments

AJ Gibson

mango
PUBLISHING

Mango Publishing
CORAL GABLES

Cover Design: Jermaine Lau
Layout & Design: Roberto Nunez
Author photo by Bradford Rogne
All other photos provided by AJ Gibson
Illustration pg. 187: Mackenzie Kuhn

For permission requests, please contact the publisher at:
Mango Publishing Group
2850 Douglas Road, 3rd Floor
Coral Gables, FL 33134 USA
info@mango.bz

For special orders, quantity sales, course adoptions and corporate sales, please email the publisher at sales@mango.bz. For trade and wholesale sales, please contact Ingram Publisher Services at customer.service@ingramcontent.com or +1.800.509.4887.

Flipping the Script: Bouncing Back From Life's Rock Bottom Moments

Library of Congress Cataloging-in-Publication number: 2018952270
ISBN: (print) 978-1-63353-830-6, (ebook) 978-1-63353-831-3
BISAC category code: SEL016000— SELF-HELP / Personal Growth / Happiness

Printed in the United States of America

For Corky—

You were the world's greatest grandma…
And then you DIED.

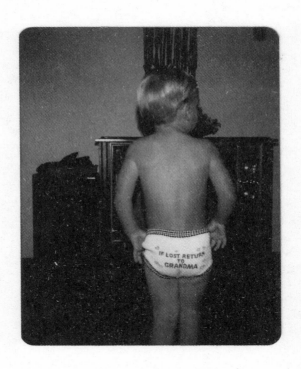

Table of Contents

INTRODUCTION:

SHAKING THINGS UP

As I sat on my toilet seat one cool October night, staring out the bathroom window of my tenth floor apartment and begging God to forgive me for the choice I was about to make, I knew I'd reached a new low. I'd struggled with depression my entire life, and the thought of ending it all had crept into my psyche more times than I could count, but I'd always been able to pull myself together and keep pushing forward. At such moments, I would weigh the pros and cons of taking my own life, and every single time I came to the same conclusion.

My life was still worth living.

This night was different, though. On this night, I could not find a single reason to live.

Sure, I knew how devastated my family and friends would be, but for the first time in my life, that wasn't enough to stop me from making what would be the last choice I'd ever make. I leaned toward the window, hands on either side of the frame and looked down. This was the closest I'd ever gotten to actually acting on my dark thoughts, and it filled me with the deepest shame I've ever experienced.

I prayed and I prayed and I prayed, and then, as if being called to do so, I looked up.

I wasn't sure why, but in that moment, it was as if I were a puppet and someone above was tugging at my strings, reminding me to focus upwards. There were quite a few stars in the sky that night—a rarity, given the brightness of the city lights of Los Angeles. And just as quickly as my gaze turned upwards, I felt a jolt to my system, followed by a sudden peace.

Moments later, I'm not even sure how, but I found myself in front of my bathroom mirror. It was at that moment, as my focus locked in on the pair of deep brown eyes staring back at me, that I knew I had two options.

One: I could head out that window, leaving my destiny unfulfilled and my loved ones to pick up the pieces that I was too broken to glue together on my own.

Two: I could look through my own eyes, deep into my soul, and work on making the changes necessary so that I never put myself in this situation again.

The two years since that night have transformed my life and opened my eyes to moments in my past that brought me to that point, and eventually, to where I am now.

This book is about that journey.

***

I'd like to introduce you to a little place that many of you may recognize: a place I like to call "rock bottom." Here, nothing seems to go right—EVER. For me, this place represents the deepest kind of despair, the type that stirs up every bit of insecurity or self-doubt I've ever experienced in life. This place makes me feel like I am unworthy of unconditional love, that maybe I am, in fact, too tall to be on TV or too broken to be successful at anything for any significant period of time. Here, in this place, I wonder if maybe God really is punishing me for being gay, and if maybe somewhere along the line, I actually did make this lifestyle choice. In this place, I believe that my dad never wanted a relationship with me because I embarrassed him and my mom only loves me because she has to (it's what moms do). My rock bottom revealed an AJ who was terrified of failure, but even more terrified of what life would look like and how others would judge him if he actually found success. To me, rock bottom represents both absolute failure AND the possibility of being able to rebuild. Until recently, I'd always accepted the failure narrative. Failing in life had always been my story, because I was too afraid to choose another path until now.

Now, I'm ready to rebuild.

This time, I've decided to shake things up. This time I've made the bold, life-changing, universe-shifting decision that the bounce back will finally be different. In the past, I've had a tendency to let my life fall completely apart and to not only hit rock bottom, but then allow myself to drag across the pavement, getting bruised and bloodied, until eventually, slowly but surely, I would kinda-sorta pull myself back up again. This was a pattern I had both mastered and accepted as my personal narrative. I was really good at playing the part of a victim in my own life and even better at justifying it to myself and others.

Everyone's idea of rock bottom looks a little different, so let me be really clear about mine. They say that tragedies come in threes, and while I'm not trying to call my rock bottom moments tragedies, they were tragic, traumatic, and not much fun AT ALL!

To kick off the worst fifteen months of my life, my baby sis came at me with some crazy new thoughts on my sexuality and knocked the wind right out of me. As the words she used to invoke Christ and judge my sexuality settled on my heart, I fell into a tailspin of despair. Not only did she judge who I am, which is the worst kind of judgment, she also judged what I was doing with my life. That was awesome! (I use sarcasm to cope, so be prepared for lots of it.) I felt awful about my soul, and now, I felt awful about the fact that after thirty-three years of struggling to find success, I'd managed to land a gig as the host of a brand-new entertainment news show on Fox. It was my dream job. I was really proud of that accomplishment and believed it was a gift from God, right up until she told me that my show was "shit" and that I was "doing nothing for Christ!" Not words you want to hear from your best friend.

Five months later I got fired from that show.

As the host of *Hollywood Today Live*, I'd felt important for the first time in my career. I had a platform to spread joy and have conversations that were meant to entertain and occasionally inspire.

The excuse I was given for why I was getting the ax was that I was "all icing and no cake." I was devastated. Immediately after being told that I was basically too shallow, my replacement was publicly announced on Variety.com and other entertainment news sites: Ross Mathews.

Getting fired sucks, but getting fired publicly and seeing the guy's face who is replacing you at the top of an article straight-up blows, especially since I'd naively suggested he fill in for me. I adore Ross immensely and have been a fan for years. He's wildly intelligent and passionate about people, and he'd been a guest on our show a few times. When I told my executive producer I was taking one day off to fly home for a long weekend and attend an Ohio State football game, I suggested they bring Ross in to fill in for me. I assumed it would be just for that one day. I assumed wrongly.

That was my second real rock bottom moment, and it was humiliating. In my mind, I was being told, "This guy is better than you." And my best friend in the world had judged both me and my show, and now I was left asking myself, "Was she right?"

Then, not long after getting canned, Uncle Sam paid me a visit, brought me to my knees, and almost sent me out the tenth story of my bathroom window. ALMOST. I'd been living off of a rapidly dwindling savings account and some residual checks from the show, all of which were disappearing quickly. I was alone, scared, and vulnerable and could not see a way out. It wasn't pretty.

So, in one tumultuous fifteen-month period, I'd learned that my sister suddenly thought I needed to pray the gay away, I had lost the job I'd worked my entire life to get, and now, because I didn't know how to manage the money I'd made while I'd been working at that job, I was in debt up to my eyeballs and alone in my bathroom, desperate to make it all end. I could take the easy way out, or I could make the decision to fight for my life. As a child, my sexuality, along with my small-town Catholic upbringing and some not-so-encouraging moments with family and friends, had all made me contemplate some pretty dark stuff more times than I can count.

But this time was different.

After some divine intervention and what I call my "Man in the Mirror" moment (I love Michael Jackson), I decided that the only way I could rewrite my story was by actually physically REWRITING my story.

I'm chatty as hell. I've been blessed with the gift of communication. For thirty-seven years I was able to get myself out of just about any situation or deflect attention from every one of my shortcomings by using some witty language and a little charm. However, without my own willingness to step up and take ownership of my life, my words were only a "get out of jail free" card. Sometimes I used them to get others to come to the rescue (they often struck a chord with my parents, for instance, who bailed me out when I was broke), but I wasn't using my words to better myself or the world around me. I was basically a young Peter Parker at the beginning of the 372 reboots of *Spider Man* that have been made so far. (Seriously, why are there so many?) He had a gift and he was reckless, until his soon-to-be-dead uncle taught him that with great power comes great responsibility. Spider Man is obviously way cooler than I am, and I'm definitely not in the business of fighting crime, but words are powerful, and I was not using mine to the best of my ability. I'm deeply ashamed of the way I've coasted on my abilities my entire life.

You see what I did there? I made myself just vulnerable enough so that you'd relate to me and then I showed you that I want to do better. I just weaseled my way out of the hole I just dug, all in an attempt to avoid your judgment. It wasn't intentional, but that's what I mean when I say words were a crutch. They've won me more arguments than I've deserved, and my words have also helped me to slither out of all sorts of accountability in my life.

I'm either a complete sociopath OR a guy who's felt judged his entire life who is finally ready to let his guard down in hopes of becoming the best version of himself that he can be. I really hope the latter is the truth, because my mom would be really disappointed to find out that her son's a sociopath. Also, I think it would bum me out a little too. I want to be the nice guy with the bright future!

Which brings me to this exact moment in my life. I'm at a crossroads and I'm shaking things up! I'm Flipping the Script on my life, rewriting my story, and inviting you to do the same wherever you see fit.

Along my journey, I've found that many people would rather live a life without meaning, struggling to make ends meet and lacking basic happiness, rather than putting in the work necessary to effect positive change in themselves and in those around them. I get it. I've been that guy, and it's no fun.

We are living in a world that is changing by the minute, and it feels like we're all trying desperately to keep up, but what exactly is it that we're trying to keep up with? I've always prided myself on being an individual and not caring what others think about me, but the truth is, I care…I care very much. Even typing this is making my heart race and my mind go to weird, scary places. I feel vulnerable and I feel uncomfortable, two feelings that usually make me pick up my iPhone and check my social media accounts. I can't count how many times per day I pick up my phone to see if I have missed a call, a text, or a new alert from Instagram, Facebook, Twitter or any number of the other ridiculous new platforms that seem to multiply like Gremlins eating chicken after midnight. If you don't get that reference, you're probably too young to realize the negative impact social media may be having on your life, so it's a good thing you're reading this book.

Now, don't get me wrong, I'm not saying that all social media is bad (except Live.me, that's seriously the worst). What I am saying is that, just like anything in life, too much of anything is never good for you. I've felt the shift in my own life and in the lives of those around me, and I'm not okay with it. I miss the days of face-to-face interaction and long phone calls with friends and family. I'll be honest, I still call my mom every day, usually multiple times, but I can't really say that about anyone else in my life. That reality makes me sad; it makes me feel disconnected, and it makes me question how we got to this place, so I'd like to explore that a bit. Also, my hope in writing this book is to share my story, as well as the stories of some really awesome people whom I love dearly, to remind you that we're all in this thing together.

Life is meant to be fun, miserable, messy, exhilarating, terrifying, frustrating, and absolutely incredible, all in the course of a single day. Much like the weather in my home state of Ohio, you never know what you're going to get hour by hour. You can embrace the constant change or you can complain about it. Either way, change is constantly happening. I say we learn how to not only expect it, but to welcome it with open arms and a big ole bear hug!

You see, what I want for you as you read this book is the same thing I want for myself: to face the self-sabotaging habits that we're all repeating on a day-to-day basis and to show you that no matter how glamorous someone else's life may seem, there's so much more story to tell than just what you see on TV, social media, or the big screen. And in the end, I hope you are inspired to take back your life and live the life you were created to live.

I know that change can be scary; maybe not in that whole afraid-to-go-to-bed-for-a-solid-year-of-your-life-after-seeing-*A-Nightmare-on-Elm-Street*-for-the-first-time kind of scary, but more an I'm-not-sure-what-living-the-life-of-my-dreams-would-actually-look-like sort of scary. Both are terrifying, but only one ends with your bloody remains being sprayed onto the ceiling from a mattress after you fall asleep with a TV casually resting on your stomach.

Spoiler alert: You're going to survive and movies are make-believe, so we're all good.

But this is not about that. THIS is about the type of scary that turns out much rosier —if you're willing to put in the work! THIS is about the type of scary that I've had to fight against and overcome every single day of my life, because I know that I have an obligation to myself and to the world to do so. Within the pages of this book, I'm genuinely writing myself out of one of the darkest periods of my life. I've decided that I need to shake things up in a big way and take a long, hard look in the mirror.

I'm sitting on a couch in a coffee shop in my hometown of Celina, Ohio, looking for the right words to speak to your heart in the way I so desperately yearn to. I have no problem connecting with the countless streams of people who keep marching their way from the order counter over to my little nook in the corner in front of the gas fireplace (seriously, I'm borderline famous in my hometown). Verbalizing my thoughts has always come easy to me, which is probably why everyone feels so comfortable stopping by for a chat. I love a good conversation, even though each one delays the writing process a little longer. These are my people and they're worth it.

This is day three of my sixteen-day writing sabbatical. The trick is putting my words into print. I come from a long line of talkers. Writing, however, is a whole other beast. But slay the beast I must!

I chose to come home to start this process because this is the place that made me into the man I am today, good, bad, and everything in between. If I'm going to share my story, this is where it all began.

My life in Los Angeles can be very exciting, don't get me wrong. Interviewing celebrities on the biggest red carpets and breaking down the latest Kardashian drama live on air in front of millions of viewers is a lot of fun and something I've fought hard to be able to do, but I want more. MY SOUL NEEDS MORE!

We were all created with a purpose and for a purpose. My soul desperately needed to find MY purpose. So I decided to start writing and go on the journey.

This book is my Hail Mary, my last-ditch effort to create the life I know I was born to live. In the chapters to come, I'm going to tear my chest open, bare my heart and soul to you, and hope you'll accept the love that I am pouring into the pages of this book. I'm dead serious when I say that I love you, I want nothing but the absolute best for you, and I will do my very best to make sure that the time you've dedicated to reading this book will be more than worth it.

Before we go all the way down this rabbit hole together, I'm just going to lay all my cards out on the table. I genuinely want you, my new friend, to know that within the pages of this book you have found a safe space, a judgment-free zone, a refuge. I've held so many emotions in for my entire life and in the process have built so many walls that it feels almost impossible to undo, but try I must!

I have the best family on the planet and love every member with all my heart, but like many families out there, some of the closest people in my life have hurt me the most and destroyed my self-confidence in ways I'm sure they're not even aware of. I feel guilty just typing that, but it is my truth, and I think it is something that will be able to help my readers. While I plan on being brutally honest about the messy family dynamics that have contributed to who I am today, I'll also take 100 percent of the blame for every mistake I've ever made in my life.

You must know I dropped out of school twice because I was entitled and allowed life to overwhelm me. I'm the guy who racked up over $50,000 worth of student loan debt and a few thousands of dollars more in credit card debt, with no way of ever repaying any of it without the help of my parents. I never took the time to fully understand the difference between 1099 and W-2 income, so it's my fault I got that tax bill the first year I made real money in my life. I made a lot of bad choices, and I've learned from them.

I told you it would be messy, but I promise to unpack this more later.

I'm going to get real honest about faith and God and sexuality and money and all of that complicated stuff that people are afraid to discuss with brutal honesty, because these are things that NEED TO BE DISCUSSED WITH BRUTAL HONESTY. I know I can't be the only person on the planet who feels like I'm misunderstood and don't belong in any of the subcategories that society has decided to box me into. So, I think we should talk about some of that. Actually, I think we should talk about ALL of it...no holds barred!

This book is going to be a wild ride, and I need to know you're down for the journey. If you're willing to go on the ride, you will learn a few things about yourself, and through the tools this book will provide, you will see a path toward a much more fulfilling, more exciting life! I'm not a licensed therapist, and my opinions are mine and mine alone, but I am an expert at one thing: BEING HUMAN! So if you're down for some real talk, human-to-human, that I know will benefit both of us, let's do this! I've waited thirty-seven years to put my mess of a life into words, and for whatever reason, felt compelled to then share these words with the world, so if nothing else, you're sure to have a good laugh at my expense, which I'm more than okay with.

The stories in this book jump around a bit, so I've assigned numbers to each "scene" to help clarify certain points in my journey. Life does not happen in a linear fashion, so I'd like this book to reflect that. In life, we rarely move forward along a straight path, so think of each chapter of this book as an expansion of who I am as a person. Also, at the end of each chapter you'll find "Script Rewrites." These are simple exercises aimed at helping YOU rewrite your story right along with me. Feel free to download your own personal "script" on my website www.AJGIBSONTV.com, so you'll have something tangible to refer back to after you've finished this book and go out into the world with a renewed confidence and passion for life! I can't rewrite your story for you, but I can show you how I was able to rewrite mine.

My hope is that you'll be able to relate to my life and that you'll find hope in my words, because I promise you this: I should not be alive, and it is only by the grace of God and lots of love from my family that I am even here today, about to pour my soul out onto these pages for you to read, dissect, and hopefully draw inspiration from. I love you, I am rooting for you, and this book is for you.

CHAPTER ONE:

FIRED AF!

Scene 58: AJ Gets Canned

EXT. VIETNAMESE NOODLE SHOP - DAY

The sun shines down on the pavement of the noodle shop parking lot. The lot is small and empty except for the single employee who steps out of the rear entrance from time to time, taking trash to the dumpster.

Steaming under the sun's rays is a Black Audi Q5, sitting alone in the middle of the quiet lot.

Two figures sit inside the car.

We ZOOM in on the car.

INT. BLACK AUDI Q5-DAY

A hand reaches for an iPhone 6, resting on the center console. The slender fingers are shaking as they reach to answer the now ringing phone.

We PAN up the arm to meet AJ, 35. A charismatic man; a man whose good looks can only be matched by his quick wit. Passionate and outspoken, his thirst for life is unmatched; although in this moment, with tears pressing to the surface of his eyes, his confidence and thirst for life have disappeared.

Beside AJ sits EMILE, AJ's boyfriend. Emile reaches a hand out to AJ and places it tenderly on his knee.

AJ answers the phone.

"Hey, what's up, boss?"

My executive producer was on the other end of the call. He'd been trying to reach me for three days, but I'd avoided him like the plague.

"Hey, AJ. How are you?"

I knew he was calling to fire me from *Hollywood Today Live*, so my emotions were all over the map.

"I'm fine, what's up?"

I WAS NOT FINE.

"Well, I'd like to meet up for coffee if you have time today," he said.

I didn't want to meet for coffee. Who the fuck wants to meet for coffee with the guy who's about to fire them from the biggest opportunity they'd ever had? I was the host of a nationally syndicated talk show on Fox, but I knew that would change the moment I met him for coffee and accepted my fate.

"Listen, we can just do this over the phone, I'm fine."

Still not fine. Not even close.

"I'd rather not, AJ, if that's okay with you."

Aaaaaaahhhhh...why was he making this so hard. Couldn't he just text "YOU'RE FIRED" or something so we could both move on with our lives? I've never been a huge fan of confrontation, and even though I'm not technically a millennial anymore, ever since they created that oddly accurate Xennial subcategory for all of us born between 1977–1983, I still would've preferred to communicate like a millennial in this situation. I was okay getting fired via text!

"Well, boss, if YOU need to do this in person for YOUR conscience, then I guess I can meet up with you in a bit."

"I do, AJ. Thank you."

I was being kind of a dick to him, but I was scared and hurting, and I did not want to hear the words I knew were about to come out of his mouth. I placed my phone back on the console, took a deep breath, and looked over at Emile. Without a word spoken, he knew.

Shaking, I started up my car. I'd spent much of my adult life driving a broke-down Chevrolet Equinox well past its prime, but I had decided to treat myself to a brand-new Audi Q5 just a few months prior to this moment in the parking lot of Absolutely Phobulous. (Such a cute name for a Vietnamese noodle shop.)

I was so proud of my Q5, but I really should've been focusing on paying off my debt.

Lacking even the most basic features, the Equinox was not the vehicle of a man on his way to the top of the entertainment industry. Two of the power windows no longer worked, the air conditioning had gone out years before, and the sunroof had been permanently ajar for about three years before I got rid of it. I was too broke to fix any of its issues, but once that Fox money started rolling in, I was ready to live in luxury. I was ready for windows that would go up AND down whenever I felt like it. I'd made it!

That Q5 was my pride and joy, and as I looked in my rearview mirror before backing out of that tiny parking lot, I hit the gas and prepared to guide my baby out into the alley. Instead, I guided her right into the wall in front of me!

I got out, checked the front bumper, and slouched back into the driver's seat, completely deflated. I was trying to keep it together but began to unravel quickly. Emile did his best to calm me, but in my mind, all I kept thinking about was the fact that I was about to be fired. Then, of course, I started to worry about how I would continue to pay for my car. Oh yeah, and how would I pay to fix the big scratch I'd just added to the front of it? How would I ever show my face in public again? What would I tell the parents who'd invested in my dream financially and emotionally all these years because I had convinced them that it would all be worth it? If I showed up for coffee, would this be the last time I ever met with an executive producer again?

I was spiraling.

Scratching my bumper on any other day would not have sent me on such a downward spiral, but piled on top of the gravity of the situation I was already up against, it was just too much. Wouldn't it be nice if we could pick and choose what fires to put out and when?

That's just not how life works, though, and at that very moment, the universe was teaching me a master class in rock bottom survival. Luckily, I was not alone.

"Boo, you are going to be just fine. This show does not define you. You are talented, and there will be other opportunities."

I have the best boyfriend ever. His name is Emile; you'll learn more about him later.

"I know. It's just that I don't actually know for sure that I'll ever work again, but I do believe in my heart that this is only the beginning. I just can't believe this is happening."

The strangest thing is that although I hadn't been happy on the show since returning to Fox only three months before, that didn't mean I was ready to walk away. *Hollywood Today Live* had started a couple of years prior as a two-minute internet segment that my soon-to-be-former co-host Kristen Brockman and I used to do called, "Hot Off the Net: LA Edition." I don't know that there was ever another edition in some other city, but I do know that literally no one ever watched our edition. Through lots of creative maneuvering spanning about two years, and more smoke and mirrors than I'd ever witnessed, that little segment was fleshed out, developed into an hour-long talk show, and eventually picked up for a six-week test run the previous summer.

Basically, this means we were given an opportunity to air our show in a handful of cities for a six-week period, and if our ratings were good enough, Fox would pick us up and expand our broadcast to households across the country. Those six weeks were one of the most exciting periods of my life. I was given the opportunity to learn and grow, both as a performer and as a human, LIVE on air. It truly was a magical time for everyone involved with our show. We were creating five hours of live television per week from a small studio on the corner of Hollywood Boulevard and Vine, and people were tuning in. We were the little engine that could!

The original hosts of *Hollywood Today Live*. Porscha Coleman, Kristen Brockman, AJ Gibson, Amanda Salas and Tanner Thomason

After the successful test run, we waited nearly a year to find out whether we were getting picked up. The wait was agonizing, but luckily, during that time, I was invited to fill in as the entertainment anchor for *Good Day LA*, also on Fox, while the regular anchor was away on maternity leave. This was another incredible opportunity to learn, to grow, and to keep my mind off of *Hollywood Today Live*. Eventually, we were picked up, I said goodbye to my new family at *Good Day LA*, and I went back to work.

This time, though, it felt different. We were no longer out just to have fun and see what happened; we were actually part of Fox's daily lineup, and we needed to pull in the ratings to justify that. What had done so well as a show with a group of young rookie hosts navigating their way through the latest entertainment and pop culture stories was now struggling to find an identity in a highly competitive daytime landscape. Being different was what had gotten us on the air, but for some reason, a bunch of corporate types thought they knew what was best and were hell-bent on making our show safe and stuffy and stale. The fun was gone. I did not enjoy this new normal. In fact, I hated it.

I think I can speak for all of my co-hosts when I say that this was not what we'd fought so hard to create. Had I just been brought on for a period of time to host this show and then been fired, that would've been one thing, but I'd helped create this show from the very beginning, and my heart was invested. I cared deeply for *Hollywood Today Live* and all of the people who worked tirelessly to get it on the air each day. I knew that hearing the words "you're fired" from my boss would mean more than losing my job; it would mean losing the TV family I'd grown to love during the past couple of years, and I wasn't ready to face that reality.

But there was no escaping my fate.

I'd agreed to meet my boss in thirty minutes at a coffee shop within walking distance of my apartment, so Emile and I drove home. He went upstairs to our place, and I walked across the street for what I like to call "The Coffee of Doom."

You may notice me using the word DOOM a few times in this book. I think it's a really funny word and lightens things up a bit when I'm talking about some stuff that really sucked.

I wanted to hate my boss, but we'd actually become good friends during our time together. As two gay men working in Hollywood, we took pride in knowing that we could have conversations in a public forum that would help members of the LGBTQ community to be seen and heard. At the time, I was one of the only openly gay men on daytime television, and we were both very much aware of the importance of that. Besides Clinton Kelly on The Chew, which has since been canceled, I'm not aware of another openly gay man in daytime television during my time on HTL.

I guess it's a good thing I'd recommended Ross fill in that one day for me; at least I wasn't getting replaced by some uber straight dude. GO GAYS!

Back to the coffee shop.

"How are you doing, AJ?" my boss asked as he greeted me with a big hug.

"I've been better."

How was this happening? What did I do wrong?

"I know. Listen, I wanted to meet and do this in person because I care about you and I wanted you to hear it from me. We've decided not to renew your contract. Friday was your last day. This is a business decision and has nothing to do with your talent. I wish the decision were up to me, but it's not."

At the time, it felt like one of those "it's not you, it's me" breakup scenarios. I let him say what he needed to say, and then I responded with some not-so-kind words about how I had thought we were in this thing together and how I'd lost respect for him when I had found out two weeks prior that I would be let go but hadn't heard a word about my fate from him. Basically, I was hurting and lashing out. It wasn't my proudest moment. I could've articulated myself a little better, but I do stand by the words I spoke to him that day, words that have since been explained far more eloquently to my now former boss. (P.S. We're friends again.)

You see, I'd known I was being replaced for two weeks leading up to this moment, yet I showed up for work each day like a pro and continued to do my job live on air for everyone to see. I wasn't allowed to show emotions or express what I was going through internally, because my job required me to be on camera. It was a pretty brutal learning experience, but I'm so proud of the way I handled myself during that time. I now count it as one of the greatest learning experiences of my life.

I did not feel that way at the time.

I remember getting a cold sore during my last week and asking my makeup artist Natalie to cover it up every single morning. I was under such intense stress that my body was physically reacting, and that's how stress manifests for me since my mom gave me my first cold sore as a young boy. My mom's a really great kisser, so it was worth it.

Also, I have a sort of twisted sense of humor, so you're going to have to decipher whether or not I really think my mom's a good kisser.

Okay, now stop thinking about me kissing my mom. You're being a weirdo!

Anyways, I made it through that final week, my integrity intact and my ego in shambles, but with a face that looked flawless, thanks to Natalie. She's an insanely talented makeup artist; she now works with Ross.

I'm not bitter.

Truthfully, she was so wonderful to me that last week, and in particular, on my final day at *Hollywood Today Live*. My agents had confirmed weeks before what I knew in my heart, so I was aware that the Friday before "The Coffee of Doom" meetup would be my last. As I packed my things and took mental snapshots of the set, the dressing room, and all the faces I knew I wouldn't be seeing again, I shared with Natalie what I knew. She immediately pulled me aside, grabbed my hands, and prayed for me. I cannot express what that meant to me; although I knew the road ahead would be bumpy, I knew that I would be okay, somehow.

What I did not know was just how bumpy things were about to get. I'd lost my job, but I was about to lose so much more.

Script Rewrites

For this chapter, I want you to think of something that was taken from you. Maybe it was a job, maybe it was a friendship, or perhaps you lost a loved one. I want you to close your eyes and remember that feeling. How old were you? What were you wearing when it happened? What do you remember about the time just before and after this loss took place? Did you change in any way afterward?

Feel free to sit with this for a bit and allow any emotions, negative or positive, to find their way back to the surface. When you feel as if you've pinpointed a particular moment that you are ready to address, you can open your eyes.

We'll get to rewriting your script in a few chapters, but for the first three, I'd simply like you to take some notes. I want you to write down every thought that just went through your mind. We'll revisit these "rock bottom" moments throughout the book, but the first step is being aware of them. It's important that we are aware of our roadblocks because it's impossible to address that which remains in the dark, so let's start dragging some skeletons out of the closet and into the light.

Together, through our shared experiences and the "Script Rewrites" sections at the end of each scene, we're going to flip the script on our lives.

CHAPTER TWO:

GAY AF!

Scene 62 : Lemonade

EXT. LARCHMONT VILLAGE - DAY

A blue sky arches above a quaint neighborhood; its snug streets are the perfect home for a number of shops shadowed by lines of perfectly manicured trees.

A mix of locals and tourists walk down the sidewalk at a relaxed pace, enjoying the warm summer afternoon and the light breeze.

A bird CHIRPS in a nearby tree and takes flight past an open window.

INT. LEMONADE RESTAURANT — DAY

Wind gently whips past the patio as diners enjoy their lunches, taking us inside to where the aromas of roasted chicken and freshly baked bread fill the restaurant.

Glasses CLINK as the wait staff attend each table.

Sitting at the side of the room is AJ, accompanied by his younger sister, Kari. Kari, a beautiful girl whose smile could charm even the roughest individual, has her hands folded neatly under her chin, her eyes looking deep into AJ's soul.

Her gaze drifts upwards to follow the approaching waiter as he lays their food down to the table.

"Yummmm, I'm OBSESSED with the braised short rib here, and this lemonade is legit perfection!"

I sipped on my drink, grateful for the opportunity to enjoy a rare meal with my little sister and marveling at the freshness of my lemonade.

There is no beverage that evokes a sense of classic Americana quite like a glass of ice-cold lemonade. Where I grew up, in Celina, Ohio, it was usually sold for twenty-five cents a cup by some schoolchildren on the side of the road during the hottest days of summer break. A couple scoops of that magical yellow sugar powder and some water out of the tap, and you were in business. In LA, though, the lemonade is a little more, ummm, bougie.

Here, lemonade is made with actual lemons and usually contains some interesting mixture of fresh mint, sliced cucumber, blood oranges, rosemary, or all of the above, because people in LA are just a little "extra." I'm totally down for "extra" when it comes to living life authentically and without regard for others' opinions of me. I am not down with "extra" when it involves the cost of my favorite summertime beverage. Also, it's basically always summertime in LA, and at $4 a pop, a guy like me has to be careful not to go broke over a once affordable indulgence.

So when my younger sister Kari asked to take me to lunch for my thirty-fifth birthday, I jumped at the opportunity to snag a meal from my favorite casual dining spot in LA...Lemonade. Yep, the restaurant is actually called Lemonade, and their food is AMAZING, especially the aforementioned short rib and the shaved Brussels sprouts! Also, they carry every combination of the actual lemonade beverage, each one of which is fantastic AND pricey. On this day, my sister was paying, and I was more than okay with that. I was about to GO IN on some short ribs!

"You wanna try a bite, sis? They're sooo good!"

I am the type of person who loves sharing great food with people. I didn't want to share my entire meal with her, of course, but I did want her to try a bite.

"I'm okay. Thanks, brother."

My sister had been trying to eliminate certain foods from her diet in an attempt to improve her gut health, so I'm pretty sure she wasn't willing to risk her comfort for a bite of short rib, regardless of how delicious I'd assured her it was. Her willpower when it comes to food is much stronger than mine.

We had the most incredible lunch, caught up on each other's lives, and even had a beautiful conversation about faith with a mother and daughter sitting next to us. God hasn't always been a dude I felt comfortable bringing up publicly, especially having grown up gay in a small farming community in middle America. As we got to know this mother and her daughter sitting next to us, it brought me back to a time when my sister and I were the daughter's age—a time before my sister revealed to me that she believed I could pray the gay away, which she was just moments away from doing that day, on my birthday.

Our childhood was awesome and we were by each other's side every step of the way. The two of us went to Catholic school as children. I loved my teachers and enjoyed learning about God and his disciples and all that fun stuff. My experience was a positive one. I cannot recall a single instance where I was taught to do anything other than love my neighbor as myself. However, the notion that I was somehow flawed and living a life of sin seemed to find its way into my psyche from the time I was very young.

I remember feeling that I was different by age five or six, and even though homosexuality wasn't outright condemned by my particular church, I knew they considered it to be a sin. People who don't understand the importance of representation fail to grasp its impact on young people in particular. I knew I was gay, but I never saw that lifestyle represented or accepted, therefore, I instinctively knew it was considered wrong. I grew up trying to fit the mold of the people and relationships that I saw around me.

I'd never been a fan of molds, and neither was my sister Kari.

On top of the lack of positive representation of the LGBTQ community in entertainment, the 1990s were a tumultuous era for the Catholic church in America. Throw in a few Catholic priest molestation scandals, and I was an absolute disaster on the inside, terrified of this secret I was trying so desperately to contain. Priests around the country were being outed as both gay and as child molesters. Suddenly, the two were synonymous with one another. These men weren't simply being condemned for being gay, but ALSO for raping innocent young boys. The issues were being conflated. If this was how the world was reacting to priests who were once beloved pillars of their communities, how would they judge the real me? I certainly wasn't a pedophile, but I knew that I was gay. From my perspective, the world was not differentiating between the two. That scared me and pushed me deeper into the closet, where I would remain for many more years.

So, while still hiding this dark secret and trying my best to pray it away each night, I pushed through my teenage years. After being confirmed at sixteen and then going away to college at eighteen, I sort of decided that it would be in my best interest emotionally to become an atheist. I was still in the closet, unable to picture a life where I survived into my twenties if anyone ever found out my deepest, darkest secret. It was such a scary time in my life that I could not even visualize what living a life as an openly gay man would look like. I'd spent so many years lying to myself and everyone around me that stepping out of the closet and into the light seemed like a fantasy. I'm not sure if I was more afraid that I might take my own life or that it would be taken from me; either way, I just knew I could not allow the world to see the awful person I believed I was inside.

This was just one year after Matthew Shepard was beaten, tied to a fence post, and left to die in the cold Colorado night, before being found the next day, when he was finally rushed to a nearby hospital. He clung to life and fought courageously, but on the fifth day, he passed. He died for being gay. I did not want that to be my story. There was one major problem: I was baptized Catholic as a newborn, and as my mom often reminded me, that meant I was to be a Catholic for life. My attempt at atheism was weak, but it allowed me to step just far enough away from the church to catch my breath and gain some perspective.

I had never been able to fathom that I could live as both a follower of Christ and a gay man, so I made the decision to step away from faith. It wasn't easy. I'd grown up volunteering with the parish nuns, collecting and crushing aluminum cans to be recycled, and doing light yard work or whatever else Sister Laura, Sister Martha, and Sister Nancy needed done outside their little nun house. I'm pretty sure there's a real term for the house they lived in, but I'm going to just roll with nun house: it sounds funny to me!

When I worked extra hard, I would sometimes get a plate of double chocolate cookies, so it was well worth it. I would sing solos in church that would melt my mother's heart, at least until my voice changed and the solos were left to Hale McKirnan. He was the coolest kid at Immaculate Conception Elementary and someone I desperately wanted to be like. Losing solos to him just about broke my heart. I decided to become an altar boy. It was the next logical step toward my long-term goal: priesthood.

Little AJ's First Communion...sister Kari was never too far away.

If this sounds crazy to you, trust me, I get it! I spent so many years fighting demons within myself that were constantly contradicting each other. Like I said, I couldn't envision a future living as my authentic self, so I thought a life of celibacy was the only way for me to survive and not end up burning in the fiery pits of hell. I used to cry myself to sleep at night, terrified that I would dream about that place. I could see myself burning for all eternity because of my sexuality, so priesthood seemed like a totally logical way to avoid that.

Now clearly, that's not how things worked out for me. The best-laid plans rarely do, but I share this story to make one thing crystal clear: God was at the center of my universe. The outside world, however, made it very clear to me that I was not, in fact, at the center of His. Over time, I decided that it would hurt less to step away than to stay in what felt like an abusive relationship. I became atheist-ish in order to survive.

Now, I was never really that good at the whole atheist thing, even though I remained in that limbo for about fifteen years. Outwardly, I was the smartest guy in the room and knew everything there was to know about the falsities of faith and everything that came along with it. Jesus wasn't born on December 25th, Noah really didn't fit two of EVERY LIVING SPECIES on that ark, and the Bible was written by a bunch of dudes. I was smarter than the suckers who still went to church on Sundays, and I let them know it. While those Christian fools were sitting in uncomfortable church pews, I was sipping on bottomless mimosas at brunch with my friends and living my best life.

At least that's how it appeared on the outside.

Inside, however, I still privately asked God to stick by me as I fought to get through life, on the odd chance that He actually did, in fact, exist. Old habits die hard, and my Catholic schooling had embedded some beliefs inside of me that would take over thirty years to adjust.

So, I secretly prayed.

At my core, I've always known that we are all a part of something much larger than ourselves and that we are connected to each other in a way that I could never explain. We share in a divinity that is mysterious and powerful and beautiful and sometimes terrifying, all at the same time. Whether we call it God, source energy, the universe, or anything else, I've always instinctively known that there is something greater than ourselves, even though I wouldn't be caught dead admitting that publicly for the entirety of my late teens to my early thirties.

As my thirty-second year began to wind down and I approached my "Jesus year," something crazy happened to me. I met a guy ten years my junior, and not only was he young, he was the black son of a preacher from the south and he was very much in the closet. Long story short, my love for him amidst the turmoil he was experiencing after coming out to the Reverend compelled me to blurt out a sentence I never thought I'd hear myself say.

"Emile, if you think it would help your parents accept our relationship and who you are, we can start going to church."

The very next day, we stepped through the doors of Mosaic, a church on the corner of Hollywood and La Brea. I was there because I loved him, or so I thought.

Within moments of the first song of worship, I was in a full-on ugly cry. I wasn't teary-eyed, I was BAWLING like a maniac, and it didn't let up for the whole service. Pastor Erwin McManus spoke that day, and it felt as if he spoke every word directly to me, even though the church was filled to capacity. Was it possible that God was using the love I had for my boyfriend to bring me home?

Yep. That's exactly what He was doing, and in just over an hour, God had erased my fifteen years of doubt by piercing my heart with the words being spoken to the congregation. I felt at home.

My stubbornness was broken, and the emotional floodgates were opening. So much so that a few months later, while my sister Kari was struggling to find happiness with her then-fiancé and making destructive life decisions, I convinced her to attend church with me one Sunday. She had stepped away from faith after graduating from college, but I wanted her to experience what I was experiencing. I had drunk the Kool-Aid, I was ALL IN, and I wanted the two of us to go on this journey together.

She showed up, she loved it, and six months later we were baptized together by my good friend Hank, who was a pastor at our church at the time as well as the first friend I'd made in Los Angeles years before. The universe seemed to finally align, and although we'd been best friends our entire life, I thought my sister and I were about to finally have the deep relationship that as an older sibling,

I'd always longed for. I thought that since we were both now adults, she'd be able to look at me and appreciate all the ways I'd guided and protected her while we were children being raised in a single-parent home. I was ready to dive deep into a relationship with God, and my sister would be by my side every step of the way. After all, she was the one person I'd trusted with every secret for as long as I could remember.

We'd moved across the country to LA together and shared an apartment for over five years, and not once in our adult lives had I ever felt an ounce of judgment from her regarding my sexuality. She had always defended me with an unmatched and unapologetic ferocity, usually against those claiming to love me while simultaneously condemning me to hell for living in "sin." I use quotations because neither of us accepted the idea that homosexuality has ever been a sin. In fact, we knew that God created me exactly as He intended me to be, and if people didn't understand that, that was their problem.

Kari and I were rock solid.

Until it was apparently her problem too, which I did not know before our afternoon at Lemonade.

We finished a beautiful, in-depth conversation with the mother and her child next to us, tossed out our trash, and walked outside to say our goodbyes. A hug, a thank you, and a short walk to my car was what I'd expected. What actually happened was much different and devastated me in ways that I'm still processing, but have since tried desperately to accept. The conversation that followed as we stood on the side of that curb outside the restaurant with the really fancy lemonade gutted me.

While the next few minutes are still a bit hazy to me, the words my sister spoke have been burned into my memory forever. I had never considered these words could actually be spoken, not by this person—not by my sister and best friend.

As I type this I can physically feel my body changing, my heart beating faster and my mind doing everything it can to convince me to shut down and turn back. I wrote the first part of this chapter weeks ago, but I have avoided finishing it because I wasn't yet emotionally ready to go back into this headspace. The problem with not sharing my story is twofold. First, by holding it in, I'm not allowing myself to learn from it, to grow and to heal. Living this way is never a good idea.

Also, I believe that my story will help someone, somewhere, so I'm fighting my internal monologue right now and laying it all out on the table. If you're reading this book and you draw strength or compassion or a sense of understanding from my story, then this will all have been worth it. So, here goes.

"I've been praying for you and I just want you to know that God loves you and that He wants more for you."

The hairs on the back of my neck stood up, because I intuitively knew where this was heading. This was not the first time someone has tried to start a conversation with me using those words. I knew the bottom was about to fall out of my life.

So in a last-ditch effort to steer the conversation off the edge of the cliff and get into my car unscathed, I responded with something like, "I know He loves me. Life's been rough, especially lately, but I know He's moving in my life and I'm excited to see where it leads."

Phew, I was in the clear!

"I know things have been difficult for you, but as I dive deeper into my faith, I've had conversations with people that have really opened my eyes."

Fuck, I didn't shake her. Here it comes!

"I just think God's plan for you might be different than you think it is. Maybe it's not for you to be gay. I've seen His love completely transforms people's lives, people just like you, if you remain open to Him."

Aaaaannnnddd there it was. My entire world crumbled in that moment; the to-go lemonade I was holding in my hand was the only thing I could feel, and my primal instincts took over.

Are you familiar with the concept of the fight-or-flight response? Well, normally I would've stood there and fought with my sister, and we would've worked it out, hugged, and moved on because that's what family does, but not this time. This time was different. This time, everything inside my soul told me to run! So I did, sort of.

In that moment, every bit of judgment I'd ever experienced came rushing back to me. Each time I'd ever been called a fag or sissy or Gay J or A Gay (since luckily both of my initials just so happen to rhyme with the word gay), each one of those words had pierced my soul like a small knife, and now, suddenly, all of those wounds had been ripped open.

I was bleeding out.

For the first time in my life, I was without words. As we've already established, I'm a man of many words, so you know how profound that statement is. I work as a TV host and public speaker for a living; communication is my thing and always has been. My grandpa used to tell me I could sell ice to an Eskimo, but just as the ice in my to-go cucumber mint lemonade was melting away, ruining the delicious beverage still in my hand, I felt my entire life melting away as well. I'd fought so hard for so many years to turn my life of lemons into lemonade, but in that brief moment on that sidewalk in Larchmont Village outside the restaurant where my baby sis had taken me to celebrate another year of life, I was left with the most sour lemon the universe had ever handed me. I was destroyed.

I got into my car, drove back to my apartment, walked into the bathroom, and sat on the toilet, seat down, pants on, for the next three hours. I didn't cry, but not because I didn't feel the need. I was so blown away by the words I'd just heard come out of my sister's mouth that I was simply numb.

You see, my sister and I were the pride of our family, and for many, the pride of our hometown. We had taken a leap of faith together, first moving to New York City, Harlem to be exact, and then to the entertainment capital of the world, Los Angeles, California. We had hopes and aspirations and dreams of taking over the industry together, because we worked best as a duo. My sexuality and our constant defense of it had actually brought us closer together. We were on the same team.

When Kari's girlfriends would complain that their brothers were jerks and just picked on them all the time, Kari would brag that I gifted her with her very first pair of Victoria's Secret thong underwear one year because she couldn't convince Mom to get them for her. I used to put her hair in curlers, because I knew how important school pictures were for her overall image, and the Richard Caruso Molecular Hairsetter was like catnip to a young gay boy growing up in a creatively stifling environment. I would spend countless hours hitting the volleyball around with her in our driveway, making her repeat "Division I" back to me each time she would bump or set the ball, because I wanted her to know that she was capable of getting a full ride scholarship at that level. She was the most phenomenal female athlete I'd ever known, and I needed her to believe in herself as much as I did because I knew we both needed to get out of the small town where we'd grown up. Our dad exited the picture when we were at a very young age, leaving me as the most important man in her life for many years. and I never wanted her to doubt for a moment that she was supported.

Well, we did get out of that small town, but as I sat on that toilet seat looking out of the tenth-story window of my two-bedroom apartment, the realization that my sister no longer supported me consumed my soul. I'd been hurt by her before, and I'd hurt her a million times, but this was different. Siblings fight, but this was more than that. Without a voice raised or a curse word hurled, my sister tore me to shreds and left me on that curb outside that restaurant on my birthday.

I spent the next three or four days sort of processing all of the emotions that kept making their way into my brain. I discussed it a little with my boyfriend Emile but didn't want to get into the details because that would've made it all too real. I avoided my mom like the plague, because I didn't want to burden her with more of our drama—God knows she'd heard enough over the years—but eventually, she called me.

Like I said earlier, my mom and I talk usually multiple times per day, often via FaceTime, or at the very minimum, through text. I call my Momma Kath (she loves that nickname) an abnormal number of times on any given day for a variety of reasons, which I'll dive into later in the book, but for the purpose of this particular story, I'll just say that it was odd not to talk for four days, and she knew it.

When the phone rang, I decided it was time to stop wallowing and answer. We made small talk for a bit, and then she asked me what was wrong. I assured her I was fine, but she knew better (because she's a mom, and they're like wizards), and so she pressed further. I wanted to handle this like an adult; I wanted to process it on my own time, and I didn't want to bring my mom into the middle of it.

"Kari thinks I can pray the gay away."

Well, that didn't exactly go as planned.

"WHAAAT?!?" She may have added a couple other words, but you get the picture.

I told her what had gone down, explained that I was trying not to drag anyone else into it and that I would be fine (because holding deep, traumatic emotions in has always worked out so well for me in the past). Then, the floodgates of my fragile mind finally burst open, and every emotion I'd carried in fear since the time I first knew I was gay as a six-year-old child came pouring out in a deluge of emotions that I could not control. The tears quickly turned into the ugly variety, and I started having trouble breathing as I uttered the words that scared me the most.

"If Kari, the person I love more than anyone on the planet, the person who has never judged me in my life, who has always had my back, can turn on me, ANYONE can. I could lose you, I could lose my other sisters, every person in my family could walk away from me if Kari can."

That realization, rational or not, felt deeply real and hit me hard. I was choking on my own words, feeling the gravity of each syllable that fell from my mouth, each more painful than the previous.

"Honey, your sister is full of shit, and if she asks me, I'll tell her that! I will never agree that you were not born gay. God does not make mistakes."

Mom generally tries to play Switzerland when it comes to sibling rivalries and arguments and rarely takes sides. This moment and the way my mom responded was definitely rare, but exactly what I needed to hear. I was broken, and had my mom responded in any other manner, I'm not sure I could've been fixed. She realized the weight of the moment and acted accordingly. I will forever be grateful to her for that.

Because of my mother's words, I was able to calm my breathing, dry my tears, and move on with my day, but I knew that my life and my relationship with my sister had changed forever. I'm sure Kari realized she'd hurt me, even though her intentions were to show me the deepest kind of love…God's love. Unfortunately, what she'd actually done was inflict the deepest wound I'd ever experienced, and she did it using the one thing that had been at the core of every bit of judgment, harassment, and depression I'd experienced in my life: Religion.

Notice that I didn't say God, because I knew in my gut that this was not God, as confused as I was at that moment and would be for the next two years. Her words were not from God. Her words were a result of human beings attempting to play God. My sister was attempting to "hate the sin, not the sinner."

If you're a member of the LGBTQ community, you know how hurtful those words are to hear. If you're a Christian who has used this phrase in an attempt to mask your judgment of others as love, just know this. Myself and my LGBTQ brothers and sisters were created by God, with purpose, for a purpose. When you try explaining your prejudice away by saying you hate our actions, when those actions are not something that can be changed, because they are a part of our DNA in the same way that your brown eyes or blonde hair are a part of yours, you create an impossible scenario from which we cannot escape. That is more traumatic than you know. So, try dropping that phrase altogether.

Now, off the pulpit and back to my sister.

I know that Kari was simply saying what she thought was best for me. I know that love was her intention, but I also know that she was misguided in her attempt to express that love. In the moment she uttered those words, and in the years since, I've often come back to the words Jesus spoke while dying on that cross: "Forgive them, for they know not what they do."

It's a beautiful approach in theory, but I am far from Christlike, and this shit hurt. It hurt bad! Sometimes, though, it takes a deep pain like this to propel us forward to the life we were created to live. So, I've tried really, really hard to forgive her for not knowing the deep impact of her words, but first, I felt sorry for myself.

For a couple of years, I wallowed. Like I had throughout my life, I accepted my role as the victim in this scenario, constantly asking God how He could let her do this to me. I wasn't getting answers. Then, I decided to act!

I decided to flip the script.

Script Rewrites

For me, this chapter is about losing a safe space and feeling judged. Has something similar ever happened to you? Can you think of a time when a relationship or situation you had considered solid or even sacred turned into something that made you feel judged or betrayed?

Again, I'd like you to close your eyes and think about that experience. What is it about that situation that cut you so deeply? Where do you think it went wrong, and what part, if any, did you play in that? Have you moved on or does this memory still carry pain?

Sit with these thoughts for a moment and allow any emotions that accompany them to pop up. We're playing an emotional game of Whack-A-Mole during these first three chapters, but for now we're simply observing the moles, allowing them to rear their ugly heads and putting those emotions into writing. After we've all established our personal rock bottom moments, then we'll get to work and start whacking, trust me!

CHAPTER THREE:

BROKE(N) AF!

Scene 66: Me & My Uncle Sam

EXT. APARTMENT COMPLEX — NIGHT

We PAN UP the side of a building to an open window of a large apartment complex; the window located ten stories above the pavement below.

The atmosphere is quiet surrounding the complex.

The only noise pervading the air is a steady flow of MUFFLED SOBS.

INT. APARTMENT COMPLEX — BATHROOM — NIGHT

A droplet of water falls from the faucet of a sink and produces a soft TINK against the porcelain base.

Sitting on the toilet, head in his hands, is AJ.

Without control, his shoulders start shaking violently as his body hunches over, lowering his head further into his lap.

He chokes out a "Dammit, AJ!" as his heels pound the tiled floor.

Tears cascade from the sides of his palms and darken his jeans upon impact.

Through spread fingers, he looks toward the open window.

Alone on my toilet, I saw no way out. Like any life, mine had been filled with a series of highs and lows which I always seemed to find a way to navigate. I'd been fired publicly from a job I thought was my big break, and I'd survived my worst nightmare coming true the moment my sister judged my sexuality for the first time, but I had been left bruised and battered along the way.

On the outside, I was strong. Inside, I was damaged and nearly destroyed.

So as I stared at the email from my tax preparer on my iPhone, I felt something coming over me that I'd never experienced before, not like this.

I was breaking.

Apparently, $16,631 was my breaking point. That was the insurmountable amount of the tax bill I'd just received and I had no idea how I would ever overcome that number. It might as well have been 16 MILLION dollars.

Uncle Sam is an asshole! Maybe it's time we consider calling him something else, like maybe "Sam the Soulsucker" or "Satan Sam," because in that moment, there was nothing familial about "Uncle" Sam.

I know A LOT about uncles, and they are NOTHING like this guy. I am one, and I have a bunch of my own; Uncle Jim, Uncle Bill, and Uncle Tom on my mom's side and then on my dad's side there's Uncle Jim, Uncle Bill… Whoa, wait! I'm just now realizing that I have a lot of uncles with the same names. Add that to the two moms I have named Kathy and the two dads named Steve, and my midwestern family is all sorts of vanilla. Also, you read that correctly, my parents Steve and Kathy divorced and then each married new partners with the same name as their previous spouse. My life is totally normal. I adjusted, but the lack of creative naming in my family will not be a tradition that will live on through me. I'm definitely naming my kids the most awesome names ever, starting with my oldest son, Blaire Jonathan. He will be a jock, possibly a ladies' man and a charmer.

The middle child, my only daughter, will be named Reagan Corinne, with Reagan pronounced like the last name of John Legend's wife Chrissy, not like the last name of the homophobic former President, because ewww. Her middle name is my grandma's first name, though she's more commonly known as Corky, a diehard Republican. So if you think about it, my daughter's name is actually quite bipartisan. Reagan Corinne will be a phenom on the volleyball court, but I'd be okay with her taking up swimming or basketball too. She could even be a cheerleader.

Finally, there's my youngest son, Brantley Michael, the sassy gay son I never was but always wished I could be. He wears what he wants, expresses himself through his art, and always has the wittiest retort to literally anything. He's the person we all regret not being in those split-second moments when we miss the opportunity for the best comeback ever, instead saying something totally lame every single time. Brantley is dope AF!

I'm far more capable of naming children than my grandparents or my parents were, even though I seem to fail miserably at the whole not-putting-unfair-expectations-on-your-unborn-children thing. I've always planned on having a family of my own, even though that didn't seem possible for so many years. There weren't many same-sex parents in northwest Ohio providing an example for me to mold my own future after, so I was never able to fully envision the HOW; for that reason, I focused on the fun stuff, like what I would name the children and how awesome they'd be.

Right now, I'm using a little humor and misdirection to take your mind off the fact that I'm sitting on my toilet seat, contemplating my own suicide. I'm not proud of that moment, and I'm not proud of the fact that I'm trying to make light of the situation right now by being witty. It's just sort of what I do.

That night was the scariest moment of my life and not one I like to think about often, but writing a book about your rock bottom moments without giving any details about the moment when you nearly ended it all isn't exactly authentic, so bear with me. I'm trying.

I remember thinking to myself how hurt my family and friends would be if I decided to jump.   Uncle Sam decided to step into my life after I'd hit my newest, lowest point. The funny thing about low points is that we always assume each point is as low as we can possibly go—until we discover that there's actually further left to fall. Uncle Sam was kind enough to teach me that lesson on a cold October night in 2016. He believed in my abilities to fall to even greater depths. Looking back, maybe I should've been more grateful for all the Uncle Bills and Uncle Jims in my life, because as I was about to find out, Uncle Sam is NOBODY'S favorite uncle!

I sat hunched over in the bathroom, defeated and overcome with shame.

Everyone knows that tax day falls on April 15th each year, unless you're broke and jobless like I was, then it falls on October 15th. You see, my delinquent ass had no idea how I was going to pay to file my taxes, let alone pay them. I'd always looked forward to tax season and the refund I thought would just come my way. After a year of making real money for the first time in my entire life, Airbnbing my spare bedroom, and earning 1099 income from which taxes were not withheld for the first time ever, my gut told me to avoid filing at all costs! So I did avoid it, until October.

The six-month extension seemed like a blessing in April and on through September, but as soon as time ran out and I couldn't avoid ole Sam any longer, shit got real. It got real to the tune of $16,631.

It may as well have been sixteen MILLION, because at that time, it would not have mattered. I was so far in debt that I could not even begin to wrap my brain around ANY dollar amount. I was living off spaghetti, butter, and Parmesan. As a child, that was my favorite carbo loading pre-swim meet meal! As an adult, it was an affordable means of survival. I still bought Kraft parmesan though; I'm not an animal!

On this Saturday night, I was home alone while my Emile waited tables. I was paying the minimums on my maxed out credit cards and on the note for a car lease I could no longer afford; meanwhile Emile was covering half the rent while I used Airbnb income to cover the rest. I was earning that money by playing housekeeper and host to random travelers from around the globe. It wasn't my preferred mode of income, especially considering that just months before, I had been the host of a daily talk show on Fox, but it was keeping food in my belly and a roof over my head. Oh, how times had changed.

The Audi Q5 that I had leased during the most financially stable period of my life, which had been a deep source of pride during my rise, had become a heavy financial burden during my steep fall. I could've leased a Hyundai or a Kia or some other perfectly fine vehicle and paid a fraction of the price, but the word Audi and those four rings across the front grill meant something to me. Actually, they meant something to the world around me, and I was okay with that, until I wasn't.

So, as I received the email from my tax preparer casually letting me know that I now owed the US Treasury Department $16,631 in addition to the $400 due in preparation fees, my world began to physically collapse around me. I was alone, I had no one to talk to, and I could see no way out. I felt intense shame while reading that email and coming to the realization that once again, I'd failed at something new. This time felt different though. This time, I knew the shit had officially hit the fan.

The rock bottom moments of the previous year had snowballed, knocking me further and further downhill, but I had been able to stop the momentum and regain my footing. This moment was pushing me to the very edge of the cliff. As I dangled precariously over that edge, staring out that window and contemplating my next move, my mind continued to spiral.

Have you seen the movie *Get Out*? If you haven't, go buy it now. If you have, then this analogy will make sense to you.

As the enormity of that dollar amount began to set in, I felt my life starting to sink. I was having difficulty catching my breath, and I felt the tears welling up in my eyes. Much as I had after my conversation that day with my sister, in life's difficult moments, I often find myself on the toilet seat, and this situation was no different. The lid was down and I was fully clothed, but there's something oddly comforting about sitting on a toilet. As a child, I remember both my father and my grandfather reading the newspaper on the toilet. Without ever being told, it's like I instinctively knew that as a man, I could find some peace and quiet on that porcelain throne. I could find refuge and a place to clear my mind.

Except this time, refuge is not what I found. This time I was overcome with a deep anxiety, the likes of which I'd never experienced. It felt like that crazy white lady from the movie *Get Out* had just stirred some tea into a porcelain mug, and I was falling deeper and deeper into despair. I had put myself into my own version of the sunken place, and I had no control over how far I was falling. The barrier holding my tears back broke, and they began to flow down my face; my breaths were becoming harder to control, and I was in full-on panic mode.

I kept glancing down at my phone, checking and rechecking that email from my tax preparer, hoping I'd misread something or that she'd sent me a follow-up email saying something like, "Oops, just kidding…you're actually getting a refund!"

That email never came.

I wanted to call my boyfriend, but he was at work and I didn't want to unload my problems on him. I'd been struggling with some pretty intense depression since being let go of *Hollywood Today Live* and since my sister had let me know how she now felt about me, so Emile had dealt with his fair share of AJ's rock bottom moments already. It's never easy to open up to your partner about things like depression and finances, and in this case, the two were intimately intertwined. I'm also ten years older than he is, so in my mind, I should've had my shit together and not needed to rely on him.

In reality, he was raised with a much stronger understanding of money and had never experienced the crippling weight of debt, so I probably should've allowed myself to lean on him a bit more. My ego was too fragile and I was too proud to consider that someone a decade younger than me could really help me through this rough patch.

Age is just a number. Don't fall for the same trap I did!

My next instinct was to call my mom, but I already owed my parents a lot of money. My stepdad Steve—or Pops, as I like to call him—would give me the shirt off his back without hesitation. One of the kindest, most generous people I've ever met, he's bailed me out more times than I can ever recall. But I was embarrassed and I felt defeated, wondering how I could be such a failure and why I seemed to be the only person on the planet who just couldn't get the whole money thing right.

So, I sat and I sank. Further and further down into my own sunken place I went, letting my mind go to places of fear I'd never considered, even in my lowest moments.

I felt as though I had no one to turn to and no options left to dig me out of this deepest, darkest hole. And then I looked out the window of my tenth-story bathroom once again and it came to me... this was my only way out.

This is where the story gets hard for me and where I'm fighting back tears just to get these words out. I'm feeling all sorts of fear, embarrassment, and shame welling up inside of me once again, recalling that night. But we can't flip the script without first writing the script, so here goes.

I was overwhelmed. A lifetime of shame and failure had caught up to me, and that email had pushed me over the edge.

$16,631. That's what it took for me to finally feel like my life was no longer worth it. $16,631 was enough to make me question my value as a son, a partner, a brother, and a friend. $16,631 was going to be the thing that finally took me out, after a lifetime of battling, of fighting for the life I'd thought God had created me for. This is what I felt I was worth: $16,631, the price of a brand-new, base model Kia Soul.

That's a shitty place to be, but that's exactly where I was.

As I sat on the toilet, I prayed and I prayed, and I prayed some more. I was spiraling, unable to catch my breath. I relived every time I'd been bullied for being gay or told that God did not make me this way. I was so sure that God was punishing me, that all the hurtful things I'd been told about myself over the years were true. I begged God to slow my heart, which felt as though it might beat its way right out of my chest, to calm my mind, and to show me a way out.

And then I realized that there was in fact a way out of this.

One that had crossed my mind before, but that I'd never ACTUALLY considered.

That bathroom window.

I was ready to end my life, right then and there. This was the end of my story.

The same window I'd stared out of contemplating the words my baby sister had spoken to me that day on the sidewalk would be the same window that would see me bring an end to my life on a cool, lonely autumn night in mid-October.

I cannot even express the deep shame I feel right now seeing those words in print in front of me, but at the time, I saw no other way out. My perspective was one of despair, and there was not a person on this planet who could have talked me out of what I was about to do. I was in a dark place. We all have our struggles, and I'm not here to compare my despair and heartache to anyone else's or to diminish what others have gone through. I'm deeply aware that for some people, something like my tax bill seems petty. But in that moment, the sum of the past fifteen months seemed insurmountable. I felt connected to the souls of those who had taken their own lives because they had no one to turn to. I was overwhelmed by the sensation of being in tune with those who had met their end tragically, well before their time.

Life has a funny way of bringing us to our knees and humbling us in preparation for life-altering messages. That night, I was being pushed to my absolute limit and brought to the end of my rope. It's almost like God needed me to see and to feel the despair of those beautiful, lost souls so that I could use that experience to shift my perspective from one of hopelessness to one of empowerment. If I could survive this new, lowest rock bottom moment of my life, then I could use this story to help others overcome their own struggles.

As I stood and sought God, hoping I'd see him staring back at me in my bathroom mirror, I saw so many things through His eyes.

In that moment, against all odds, my life was given purpose.

I am here to love, I am here to share, and I am here to encourage. It is only by the grace of God that I still exist, so it's like I'm living on borrowed time, and I will not waste another minute of it—and neither should you.

In that moment, I knew why I had to keep fighting for my life and for my happiness:

You.

YOU are my purpose!

The reality is that every minute of every life is actually lived on borrowed time, but we tend not to learn that lesson until the prospect of "the end" creeps into our lives. Sometimes the lessons are small—like the forty-five minutes I was convinced I had a brain tumor—and sometimes the lessons are large and terrifying, like that lonely night in October.

But the lesson remains the same: You are worth it.

Your life has meaning, and there is no dollar amount that could ever be placed on your existence.

Whatever the struggle, there is a way out. It may not be a way that you're willing to take, because it's probably going to be scary and difficult and force you to face truths long ignored, but if you're willing to make the shift, your life will grow.

Uncle Sam is not someone I wanted to know, and he's still not someone to whom I prefer to give too much of my time, but he taught me a deeply powerful lesson. I am divinely created, you are divinely created, and we are all meant to live together, and to share our failures as freely as our triumphs. It's easy to brag about our mountaintop moments, but it's those moments where we hit rock bottom, where we are at our absolute lowest, that hold the most power, because in those moments, truly anything is possible! As humans, when our backs are against the wall, we have two choices. We can either slump down, put our hands over our faces, and hope whatever is backing us into a corner simply disappears.

Or we can come out swinging!

Retreating always leads to the same result, which involves no growth and a zero percent chance of a happy ending, so what's the fun in that? There is none. So why not come out swinging and fight for the life you were created to live? The result may surprise you.

I chose to fight for my life.

Retreating was not an option, and as I felt the love of those whose lives were cut short too soon, those who felt they were not strong enough to fight, I also felt the love of every single person on this planet who cares for and adores me…who is rooting for me to succeed! All of the Kathys and Steves and Bills and Jims—and even the Sams in my life! I owed it to them to fight through this moment of despair, to learn from it, and to use it to help others who might be going through their own $16,631 moment. Also, I knew that I'd never get the chance to meet Blaire, Reagan, or Brantley if I decided to throw in the towel that night, and that was not something I was okay with.

Straight folks get to have unplanned babies all the time, my dad did it five times with three different wives. For me, the road is much longer and requires time, money, and preparation, none of which could happen if I were to end up lifeless on the pavement outside my window.

I will be a father someday, and although the names may change and the lives of my unborn children will play out in ways I could never foresee, I have to exist for their future to manifest.

Also, stay on top of your finances and pay your taxes on time. Uncle Sam is no joke!

10/15/16, 11:37 PM

Patti just told me I owe $16,000 in taxes & I want to jump out the window. Obviously not, but overwhelmed right now.

10/16/16, 3:40 AM

Reading the Bible & doing some praying. Gonna stay on the couch for a while & let my mind & heart settle. I just need some time with my thoughts. I love you.

10/16/16, 4:50 AM

Was just about to come look for you but just saw this text. Love you so much. God has not forgotten about you and I know it's natural for our human brain to want to give up and not trust but opportunities come out of nowhere when we truly just believe and trust him. Stepping out on faith is scary when you haven't really seen the reward yet but it will be worth it. You are so talented and I know that God is working extra hard to bring you a blessing you can't imagine. Alright, going back to sleep. Love you

Emile saved this conversation from the night I almost took my life, because he said he knew I'd use it for something positive some day. I love that man.

Script Rewrites

I almost didn't make it through that night in my bathroom, yet it has become one of the proudest moments of my life. Writing this chapter wasn't easy, but putting into words what I went through that night and the circumstances that brought my life to that crossroads has been empowering. My story could've gone in a very different direction, but I was able to rewrite it in real time— and you can too. I don't know about you, but I'm pretty stubborn, so it took an extreme experience to teach me a lesson I was unwilling to seek out and learn on my own. This was the lesson: YOU ARE EXACTLY WHO YOU ARE MEANT TO BE!

We spend so much time worrying about what other people think about us, accepting lies about ourselves, and comparing our situation to those living the type of life we think we're supposed to be living, but the truth is that until we accept the fact that our journey is ours and ours alone, happiness will always be an idea we're chasing. Owning this simple yet complex truth is the only way through life's toughest moments. By flipping the script on a single moment in your life, you can change the course of history. THAT is how powerful your decisions are!

When life gets bad—like really, REALLY bad— you have two choices. You can accept all the awful things that are happening to and around you as truth and throw in the towel. Or you can stop, take a deep breath, remind yourself that you create your reality, and ask yourself what lesson the universe is trying to teach you. What message are you blocking yourself from receiving?

This might seem easier said than done, but I promise you it's possible. If you're going through one of those moments right now, know that I am sending you my love and hear this— YOU ARE GOING TO BE OKAY. You may not receive the outcome you're hoping for, but if it's a situation where you have air in your lungs and the opportunity to live, you've still got a chance to grow. Live in the moment, embrace the opportunity, and ask yourself what would truly make you happy moving forward; not what seems realistic or easy, but what will fulfill you and give your life purpose. If you can get quiet and real honest with yourself, the answer will find its way to you, and it might even surprise you.

I never thought in a million years that I'd be sitting here sharing this story for everyone to read, yet that's exactly what I'm doing. That moment was so scary because I was humiliated and felt like a complete and utter failure. Those aren't exactly the stories you brag to your buddies about at the gym, but they are the types of stories that have the power to give hope to others, and that is way cooler than the alternative. Anyways, what if I had jumped out the window and *survived*? I only live ten stories up, so that was possible. How embarrassing would that be! Not only was I a loser for not taking care of my shit financially, but then I'd be the guy in debt who wasn't even smart enough to kill himself properly—and I'm way too vain for that to be my story!

For this exercise, I want you to think about your support system. Who are the five people who you could call in a moment of despair? Who would be there for you in a crisis? Write those names down. We'll come back to them later.

CHAPTER FOUR:

AJ AF!

Scene 5: The Making of AJ

EXT. BITTERSWEET DRIVE

We OPEN on a street sign titled
BITTERSWEET DRIVE.

We CLOSE IN on a small house surrounded
by cut green grass and a cracked pavement
sidewalk leading up to the front door.

INT. HOUSE - LIVING ROOM

A little hand grips a spoon, stirring a
creamy mixture within a repurposed plastic
margarine bowl.

We PAN back from the small hands to meet AJ
as a child, sitting next to his older brother
and sister, Scott and Chris.

The three hold their ice cream up to the
black, wood-burning stove to speed up the
melting process.

The siblings use their spoons to create peaks
of half melted ice cream that they refer to
as "birthday candles."

The living room's decor is very late '70s
vintage. The dingy, rust color of the carpet
is reminiscent of red clay soil.

The ice cream reaches the proper consistency
and the three dig in.

Little AJ was in constant awe of his older siblings. I wanted to be like them, I wanted to be around them, and I wanted do everything they did. I was a typical baby brother in some ways.

My mom often jokes that she suffers from Half-Zheimer's, because she remembers about half of everything that she's experienced in life. Mental health is not something to joke about, but my mom literally does forget 50 percent of everything, so don't get all worked up over a few words, this isn't that kind of book. And to be honest, I'm 99 percent sure she has no idea that the actual condition is even spelled Alzheimer's, not All Zheimer's, so let's cut the woman some slack.

Or not. If you wanna make fun of her, she probably won't remember anyway, so it's your call.

Me, I remember everything. I was probably four years old when I sat next to that wood-burning stove with my older brother and sister, melting our ice cream, and I remember it like it was yesterday. I've always been that way, which is probably why recalling stories from my childhood comes so naturally to me.

It's also why I remember so vividly the moment our first dog "went to live on a farm" around the same time. I didn't find out until years later that my dad had actually run over buddy #1 with his pickup truck. It was an accident, of course, but all I remember from that day is walking to the screen door of our little house to see what all the fuss was about and my siblings stopping and distracting me while our dad apparently peeled our family pet off the pavement.

Little AJ in the truck that "murdered" Buddy #1.

Those same siblings also attended to me months later when I got clocked in the head by a fire log while my dad unloaded that same truck. As always, I'd wanted in on the action but was really just getting in the way. My dad warned me several times, but my stubbornness had already developed by that age, so I ignored him until he got my attention —with a log!

This too was an accident, I think. Just like with my mom's understanding of the origin of the word Alzheimer's, I'm 99 percent sure my dad wasn't trying to knock me out on purpose, even though I'm sure I was annoying the hell out of him that day. Either way, he clocked me right on the noggin, and I still have the scar to prove it. I wear it with pride. That scar is the first of many battle wounds I've accumulated over the years, most of which are internal and only seen by a select few whom I allow close enough to really get to know me.

Also, I am an absurdly observant human being, always have been.

It's my first memory of truly being coddled. I'm sure my parents were annoyed that I hadn't heeded their warnings and gotten out of the way, but the moment that log struck my forehead, my mom and older sister Chris sprang into caretaker mode. This is my very first memory of being nurtured, one that has stuck with me for the over thirty years since.

On that day, I learned that even when mistakes are made, a family comes together in a crisis. My forehead was in crisis, and my family took action.

From the beginning, I knew that I was loved. My parents didn't always get along and would split just a few short years later, but I always knew that I would be taken care of. In spite of their split, I knew that family would always come first.

Instinctively, I've always known that I was different. I'm not just talking about the gay thing here, although that is one of the ways society has pegged me as being different, I'm talking about the way I perceive everything around me. From people to situations and everything in between, I'm always observing and measuring. Little AJ was no different.

When I was maybe five or six, I remember sitting in our family station wagon with my older brother and sister in the parking lot outside of our local Radio Shack. Our parents had been arguing, so there was a collective tension in the air. I guess Radio Shack must have sold Atari games back then, because my siblings had asked for a new one and been shut down by our parents. The moment Mom and Dad got out of the car, I was a sitting duck.

"Ever since you were born, we never get new video games anymore. I wish you'd never been born at all!"

My brother was still a kid at the time, maybe thirteen or fourteen, so I don't blame him for feeling that way anymore, but at the time, those words hurt. As a child, I processed his words as, "I hate you, I wish you weren't alive, and you are the reason everything is going wrong in our family."

Our parents fought all the time and were near the end of their marriage, so his words impacted me differently than they would have had things been a little rosier on the home front. For so many years, I held onto small moments like that. I internalized such guilt over my parents' divorce, as if I'd somehow caused it. My brother and sister were just doing what older brothers and sisters do, but to me it felt different. Those words felt true. I knew my personal truth could one day tear my family apart, so I protected that secret.

Okay, maybe I wasn't protecting that secret as well as I'd thought, OR I was a young crusader against gender norms and toxic masculinity!

This way of thinking started a pattern that would take hold of my life for nearly thirty years. More often than not, I've taken ownership of far more than I should. It's not a healthy habit to create, but as a child, so much of what was going on around me felt like a direct result of my existence, and my brother's words that day only reaffirmed that belief.

It's funny how a simple phrase that I know my brother forgot about moments after uttering it has stuck with me for over three decades. Not funny like "ha ha," but funny like, "That's a shitty thing to say, and I can't wait to spend the next thirty years carrying the burden of your off-the-cuff remark as my own personal baggage."

Scott, I know you didn't mean those words the way I received them, and I know my brain is borderline crazy, but I'm being as transparent as I can be here, so just know that I love you and don't blame you for a thing.

Well, I definitely blame you for that time you murdered those baby bunny rabbits we found in the VFW parking lot behind our house when we were little. That was cruel, and I DEFINITELY blame you for it.

Side note: While Emile was helping me edit this chapter, he said, "This is funny, but what is 'VFW'? Can you tell us in parentheses for those who didn't grow up in Ohio?"

He's adorable.

It stands for Veterans of Foreign Wars, and it's sort of similar to the American Legion or to a Moose Lodge. Basically, it's a place where you go up to a door with one-way mirrored glass and you ring a bell so that someone can buzz you in. You have to be a member, but once you're in, you can drink canned beer and eat fried food to your heart's content. Oh yeah, there are a lot of American flags hanging everywhere, and they sell a lot of those little gambling ticket things where you unfold one end to see if you win cash. In small towns, this is where the adults spend their evenings and where EVERYONE has their wedding reception.

I've spent my fair share of time in each establishment and made some great memories. I'm totally taking Emile to one the next time we go to my hometown. Lucky for him, Celina, Ohio, has all three!

Back to the story about my murderous older brother.

That day wasn't exactly a high point for him, but I am quite proud that he didn't make a habit out of that sort of behavior, because I've seen enough documentaries to know that's TOTALLY how serial killers get their start. So Scott, I'm so proud of you for not becoming a serial killer! That would've probably led to way more emotional baggage for me to unpack, so thanks for not burdening me with that. The bunny rabbit thing did really suck, though, but the video game thing, totally not your fault!

As I share these stories of events that impacted and molded my character at a very young age, I'm aware of how illogical some of these reactions might seem, but I also know how illogical life can be. Our brains comprehend information based on our individual life experiences, and through that process, oftentimes unknowingly, we start forming patterns that, over time, feel like truth. The longer we allow these patterns to form, the more difficult it becomes to distinguish actual truth from perceived truth. That is a lesson I'm learning as I write this book.

By the time I was about nine years old, our parents had officially divorced.

They gathered the entire family in the living room of our humble home on Grand Avenue to tell us as a family. My big sister Chris held me on her lap while I held Kari on mine. We were all squeezed into a single recliner as our big brother Scott stood behind us. I was young, but I knew exactly what was happening; I was an oddly intuitive kid. Our parents stood before us in our living room, just in front of the TV.

"Kari and AJ," Mom said, "you're going to be living with me."

I was being torn from my older siblings and had no say in the matter. Scott and Chris were actually my dad's kids from his first marriage; my mom was his third wife. Their mother had died of cancer when they were one and two, and their first stepmom used to lock them in a closet while my dad went to work, so my mom was essentially the only mom they'd ever really known.

The thought of not seeing my dad, brother, and older sister every day terrified me, and in that moment, I grew up long before I was ready to. This event and the time period just before and after it have impacted my life more than anything else I've experienced. Divorce is no joke, and although I spent years convinced that I wasn't affected, it's now clear to me that couldn't have been further from the truth.

The moment they split, I became the man of the house and took on the role of protecting both my mom and more importantly, my sister Kari. It's a role that I cherished for the next three decades, but also one that altered the course of my life completely in ways I was not even aware of until recently. It became my responsibility to make sure that the women in my life were taken care of. Now, as a little boy, I wasn't about to go out and get a job, so I supported my mom and sister the only way I knew how: emotionally.

I became the backbone of the family. For nearly thirty years, my role wouldn't change all that much. My mom did eventually move on, meet a great guy, and marry him (the other Steve, a.k.a. Pops), but in my own mind, I would always be the one and only true man of the house. In my mind, my real dad had walked out on us, so what on earth would convince me that my stepdad wouldn't someday do the same? The answer: nothing.

This is a picture of me crying after walking my mom down the aisle on her wedding day. I was devastated that Kari and I no longer had the same last name as our mom, so I locked myself in the bathroom for an hour that day; that may have been a bit dramatic. Also, my Uncle Jim isn't nearly as creepy as he appears in the background of this photo!

Although the new man in our lives was doing just about everything right, I still held onto a certain degree of skepticism, because my mom and sister's well-being depended on it. That may have been 100 percent untrue, but that didn't matter to me. He did everything right. He was kind to my sister and me, and he made our mom happy, but I'd become the man of the family by then and wasn't ready for that to change. The guy even bought me an Easy-Bake Oven for Christmas that first year, yet I still wasn't ready to accept him in with open arms. Okay, maybe he shouldn't have wrapped the gift in cheap, white wrapping paper, because I totally knew what it was before I even opened it, but he was a bachelor raising three kids of his own, so the fact that he even wrapped it should probably be commended. I was around nine years old, and as badly as I'd wanted that Easy-Bake Oven, it didn't mean I was ready for a new dad.

Also, the whole idea of accepting another man into my life named Steve, just like my dad, was all too much to process, and I was a stubborn kid.

I am my mother's son.

I made some bomb-ass brownies in that Easy-Bake Oven though!

As for the "other" man in my mom's life, it would take more than a flashy gift to earn my trust!

What I didn't realize in those early years is that while I was taking on a great responsibility, I was also taking on all of my mom's bullshit and my baby sister's as well. My mom was broken by the divorce and insecure. She was still a great mom to us, but she was understandably different. My sister was the baby of the family and the center of everyone's universe, including mine. Unhealthy patterns were established in those early years that would continue for decades to come. I see that now, but back then, I was happy to do whatever I could to protect the women in my life. I wanted my mom to be happy and I wanted to keep my sister safe, so I did everything I could to make sure those things happened, regardless of the personal cost to me. As I got older, I realized that I simply couldn't do it anymore. It wasn't healthy for me, and it wasn't healthy for either of them.

In those early years, the concept of boundaries wasn't really something anyone talked about in rural Ohio and certainly not in our family. Oprah wasn't living her best life just yet, and Will Smith wasn't on Instagram, so I wasn't receiving the information I needed to create a healthier environment for myself. Also, if you don't follow both of them on Instagram yet, go do it now! Their words have a way of piercing through my thick skull and landing directly on my brain in a way that sticks; they truly are brilliant.

I now know that my day-to-day life wasn't all that different from the lives of most kids. My mom was raising two children all by herself, working in a factory and enlisting the help of our grandma Corky, who conveniently lived two doors down at the time. Also, our grandma was alive then, which certainly helped. (P.S. She's dead now. Well, because she died. We'll get to that later.)

I knew that I was loved, and I understood the importance of family, but I was not aware of the importance of self-love. That would come back to bite me in the ass as an adult.

To this day, Kari doesn't remember our parents ever being married, which is probably why she's experienced so little deferred trauma from that period of our lives. She was about four when they split, so not much in her world changed.

For me, it was during this part of my life that I became an intense people-pleaser and a nurturer. I'm still not sure where the people-pleasing thing came from, but the nurturing stuff came directly from the heart and soul of our family: my grandma Corky, before she, you know, died.

Granny C, as we often called her, short for Corinne, was the glue that held our family together. She was the perfect balance of strength, compassion, and grace. I idolized her and looked to her for guidance at a time when my mom, now raising two kids as a single mother while working third shift in a factory, was doing everything she could to just keep our family afloat. Grandma was my safe space; she was the calm at the center of the storm that had become our family life.

Conveniently, my grandparents lived two doors down from our own house, so Granny C was always just a short walk away. While mom worked five nights a week, Kari and I would sleep at our grandparents' house. We shared a room in the basement. There were actually three bedrooms down there, but one had both a really creepy oil painting of John Wayne hanging on one wall and a poster of Uncle Sam pointing with the words "We Want You" on the other.

You see, Uncle Sam had set his sights on me years ago; there was really nothing I could've done to escape him.

Well, I guess I could've paid my taxes, but then I wouldn't have this ironic plot point to share with you, so thanks Uncle Sam, you bastard!

As kids though, years before money would ever make its way onto our radar, we were far more afraid of the creepy John Wayne painting. No matter where we would go, he was ALWAYS staring right at us.

NO THANKS, COWBOY!

The second bedroom had a tanning bed in it. My grandma was a bit of a trailblazer and had run a tanning salon out of her basement for a few years, and after going out of business, she had decided to hold onto one of the beds for personal use. Tan N Glow was only the second tanning salon to open in our county in the mid-1980s, and even though it didn't last long, it showcases perfectly the type of woman my grandma was. Sure, she was helping people develop skin cancer, but she was an entrepreneur, dammit!

Also, no one really knew about that whole cancer from tanning beds thing until years later, so I don't hold that against her.

So sharing a room seemed like the best option for my sister and me. It was a far better option than having to sleep with one eye open or waking up with leathery, cancerous skin.

Side note: Tanning beds are bad, and you should always use sunscreen when you spend any significant amount of time outdoors. I felt compelled to say that.

Our mom won custody of Kari and me, because we were totally a prize to be won, so we stayed with her for the most part. Every other weekend was spent at our dad's house. Since our mom worked third shift, this meant we only actually slept in our own beds the other two weekends of the month. Five nights a week, we were at our grandparents'. As our schedules were thrown into chaos and we were being passed around every few days, my sister and I bonded in a way most siblings never do. Even in our own home, a house with four bedrooms, we preferred to share. We relied on each other and I liked feeling important. I would prove the beliefs I'd accepted after my brother's statement outside of Radio Shack to be false. I would protect my sister, and she would never feel the way he'd made me feel.

We never really talked about the divorce as children and weren't aware of the impact it was actually having on us. Kari had the luxury of ignorance, having been too young to remember a time when our family was a single unit.

I had a very different experience.

It would've been nice to have talked things through with a family counselor or maybe a priest at our church, but counseling wasn't something people in rural Ohio were big proponents of in the late eighties, and the Catholic church wasn't exactly a big fan of divorce. So I was left to deal with the repercussions of my parents' decision on my own, and I did the best that I could. The most clear way that I could see value in myself was as an older brother to my baby sister Kari, so that's what I focused on.

Being her big brother has been the greatest honor of my life. However, it has also been the source
of the deepest pain I've ever known. Fortunately, it's molded me into the man I am today, and I am thankful for it all. My older siblings impacted me and I impacted her. How we all choose to love each other as adults is up to each of us. I never had to forgive my brother, because I know his words were that of a kid. I'm trying to forgive my sister; her words were spoken as an adult.

I'm trying to rewrite our story because I need us to be okay.

She's embedded in my DNA, in my soul.

I love her, and I'm working on finding a way to fix us. I need my baby sister back in my life.

Script Rewrites

Are there stories you've been telling
yourself since childhood that were never
really true to begin with? I'm willing to
guess the answer is yes, so I've got an
idea that could really help you rewrite the
narrative, but it's probably going to make
you a bit uncomfortable.

I'd like you to contact a family member or
close friend who has played an important role
in shaping the person that you are now. I'd
like you to write down ten questions and then
set up an interview with them. I want you
to think about things you've always wanted
to know but have never had the courage to
ask. These don't need to be deep, thoughtful
questions, but some of them certainly can be.

I want you to use this as an opportunity to
gather information about a moment in your
life when this person had a negative impact
on you. I want you to approach this from a
place of love and with a student mentality.
Also, I'd like you let this person know that
they can ask you questions as well.

Record this "interview" on your phone or
some other recording device so that you
can revisit it. Write the answers in your
script and examine how their truth differs
from yours. I want you to really consider
how their perspective of the same memory
varies from yours so that you can come to a
place of understanding and mutual respect.
Then, I'd like you to have a conversation
with this person about these differences
and forgive them for any hurt they may have
caused you, as well as apologize for any hurt

you may have caused them. After that, write a few sentences about how this exercise made you feel and read it out loud to yourself. Good luck.

CHAPTER FIVE:

DUBIOUS AF

Scene 22: Who Do You Think You Are?

EXT. DRIVEWAY

The stars in the sky twinkle above a group of TEENS gathered together in a circle in the driveway of a large house.

Fireflies hover around the kids, occasionally lighting the kids' features with their glow.

Besides the house, there is nothing along the road but miles upon miles of open fields and endless rows of corn stalks.

Off in the distance are multiple silhouettes of barns, but against the night sky they are hardly visible.

Within the group is AJ, now in his late teens. Tall and lanky, he stands much higher than the rest of his comrades in the circle.

"Can you guys believe this is our last night together? Like, this is it."

This was it.

Ben was going to join a fraternity and be cool forever, Hiedi (yes, that's how she spells it) was going to make it big on Broadway, Jenna was off to cosmetology school, Jeff was headed to Ohio University to be artsy, Adam and the other Heidi (spelled the normal way) were going to be together forever, and AJ, well...AJ had no clue what he was going to do with his life. AJ had no specific plans for life after college; AJ just wanted to make it TO college. AJ wasn't raised to dream big or to establish any sort of real game plan for success, and he certainly never believed he'd one day be living in LA, working in television, and writing a book about himself in the third person, because that's just the most obnoxious thing ever.

AJ lacked direction, but that didn't mean AJ didn't have dreams. AJ has ALWAYS been a dreamer.

As I stood in my friend Phil Jutte's driveway saying goodbye to the only friends I'd ever known, I felt inadequate and unprepared for life after graduation. My friends all seemed to have their futures mapped out while all I could think about was how crazy my dreams were and how I could never share them without getting laughed at.

Turns out I was right.

It was August of 1999 and I was nineteen. I was enjoying the last moments of the only life I'd ever known as my friends and I got together one last time before each of us headed off in different directions, to separate colleges spread across the state. I don't remember talking about our hopes and dreams much up until that point. For the most part, we were focused on playing sports, partying, and getting out of what felt like the smallest town on the planet. Celina, Ohio, population 11,042, was the center of our universe, but we all knew that was about to change forever.

Growing up in a small farming community, or in any small town, can certainly have its perks. I knew every single person I went to high school with, it was easier to make the front page of the sports section in *The Daily Standard* (our local newspaper), and there was a comfortable consistency that accompanied the simple life we'd known. We felt safe, and we always knew what to expect, because nothing ever changed...EVER. Except I never truly felt safe. I knew that if my truth were ever revealed, people would have a major problem with it.

From about the time I hit puberty and realized I could not live my truth in that place, I had hated everything about it and wanted nothing more than to get far, far away and never look back. My closeted little gay self was ready for the big city, where my larger-than-life aspirations could come true and where I could finally meet the man of my dreams and have my first REAL kiss! I knew there must be other people like me out there, I just hadn't met them yet. At the time, my perspective was that small-town life was only for hillbillies, uneducated simple types. This belief was supported by the racist, sexist, and homophobic language that often seemed to go unchecked there. In my high school, pickup trucks were pretty common. Farming is the heart of the community, so driving a pickup truck made sense for that lifestyle, but what didn't make sense were the Confederate flags that often hung in the back window of some of those trucks.

I grew up with classmates proudly showcasing a flag that represents the belief that black people were equal to animals and could be hung from a tree with no repercussions simply because of the color of their skin. Supporting something like LGBTQ rights or a woman's right to choose was never an option, yet young boys were allowed to showcase that flag. The ironic thing is that Ohio was two states north of the Mason-Dixon Line and had never been part of the Confederacy. How no one ever seemed to question flying that flag is still beyond my comprehension. So for much of my youth and into my late twenties, I viewed most people in my hometown with deep judgment.

I remember in my high school government teacher Bill Sell's classroom an old newspaper clipping hung, bragging that our county had decades before hosted one of the largest gatherings of the Ku Klux Klan in the nation, and I recall being utterly repulsed by that. He'd posted it as a reminder of the hatred than can exist when we don't treat others with respect, but having been exposed to that information, along with the fact that Confederate flags were allowed on school property by administrators, and on top of my personal fears as a closeted gay teen, I'd made up my mind that I did NOT want to be like the people from my hometown.

Over the years I've come to realize that not all small-town folks are ignorant or hateful—quite the opposite, actually. I now see the deep pride and the closeness of my hometown and others like it as something quite special, especially in a world consumed by technology. I don't think nineteen-year-old AJ ever could've understood that.

Some of them still have some serious work to do on social issues, though, so they're not completely off the hook. When I took Emile home and we went to the Mercer County fair a couple of summers ago, right next to the booth aimed at electing Donald Trump President was another booth selling Confederate flags the size of a house. Coincidence? Maybe. Acceptable? Absolutely not.

None of my friends were fans of the Confederacy, thank God!

A few nights before the first of our group packed up and headed off to college, we all got together at my friend Phil's house out in the country for one final hang. It was usually easier to get away with drinking at friends' houses that were out in the country, because the local cops didn't have jurisdiction there, and if a party were to be busted, it was easier to outrun the sheriff through the woods or in a car on the backroads. I'm not condoning drinking and driving because that's just about the dumbest choice anyone could ever make, but I'm also not going to pretend none of us ever did it back then. We were a pretty good group of kids, but we were still kids, and sometimes we were very, very dumb.

This evening was pretty tame. I don't think a drop of alcohol was even involved, which is probably why I remember the night so clearly almost twenty years later. We were all standing in a circle, sharing our hopes for our futures and promising we'd always stay best friends. Like I said, this was not common practice for us, but I think the gravity of the moment was setting in. This would be our last night together as small-town friends, and we were getting the most out of these final moments.

Everyone had a plan, and so I stayed quiet, until I didn't.

"I want to move to New York or LA and become a famous actor or maybe the next David Letterman."

I was dead serious.

I'd written a paper about wanting to take over David Letterman's job someday, but that was way back in junior high, and I don't think I'd ever actually articulated that dream to anyone in the years following that bold declaration. As vulnerable as I felt in that moment, it felt awesome to blurt out my aspirations for all the world to hear. Well, my friends were my entire world at that moment, but the reaction I got from them quickly brought me back down to reality—to their reality.

"But you didn't even do any of the school musicals or plays, how do you think YOU'RE going to become famous?" Phil asked.

He's one of the nicest human beings on the planet, which is probably why his words stung. He'd also performed in all of our school's theatrical productions, so maybe he thought his question was practical; maybe it was.

That's not the way I received it.

That question knocked the wind out of me. My friends were all theater kids, but I grew up in a sports family. My mom was a high school all-American in both basketball and volleyball back in the mid-seventies, so she raised us the only way she knew how: as athletes. I excelled at track and field; I was a hurdler and really pretty badass at it. I was the Western Buckeye League champion my senior year and the district runner-up in the state of Ohio. I used to glide over those hurdles like a gazelle escaping a pack of lions in the Serengeti. I was fast!

I was a solid swimmer, too. I swam competitively for ten years, mostly because it came naturally to me and my butt looked great in a Speedo (still does). As much as I loved playing sports and competing, I knew that I wasn't good enough to make a career of it, so I'd started putting serious thought into what I actually wanted to do with my life after graduation, and since I've never been a fan of the traditional 9-to-5 work model, I set my sights on a career in entertainment.

My friends clearly didn't see the vision.

I'd never really considered that my dreams might be unrealistic until that moment in Phil's driveway. To be fair, I don't think he meant to belittle me when he asked the question, and I know that none of my friends intended to hurt me by laughing along, but no one spoke up to support me either, and I didn't like that. My friends wanted me to play small, but I knew that would benefit no one, most importantly myself, because I was at the center of my own universe back then.

I was nineteen. Don't judge me.

It would be wonderful if I could tell you some inspirational story about how I picked myself up and against all odds became a huge overnight success, but this isn't that kind of book, and that's not how success works for most people anyways. That moment stuck with me. That moment repeated in my brain for many years. That moment set me on a path to THIS moment. It made an imprint on me and impacted my belief in myself, but it also sent me on a path toward writing this book. From that point forward, I started to doubt myself a little more each time someone questioned my dreams or my goals, always wondering if my friends had maybe known something I didn't. As much as I told myself that I was a fighter and that I would use that moment to drive me, to motivate me to soar higher than anyone had ever soared before, that's not exactly how it all played out. That moment motivated me at times, but more often than not, that moment made me doubt myself.

There's a saying in Hollywood that overnight success takes ten years, and I used to buy into that mindset. What I've learned is that by accepting that as truth, we often give ourselves a pass. Personal and professional growth do not exist without pressure, and a ten-year timeline for success isn't exactly a pressure-inducing scenario. Just because someone else's path might have been long and winding, that does not mean yours needs to be the same. You can find success and happiness right now. Too often we excuse ourselves for not achieving something great or not even attempting something new, because we think we can't be the exception.

"Who do you think YOU are?"

I couldn't believe that one of my longest childhood friends had just questioned my dream like this. Phil and I had known each other since his family moved to Celina and he'd started attending Immaculate Conception Elementary with me. We played CYO (Christian Youth Organization...Emile didn't know this one either, abbreviations must not be his thing) basketball together, spent weekends at each other's houses, and remained friends through graduation. We'd grown apart some by the time we finished high school, but I was standing there in his driveway the night before we all started moving away, so there was still a relationship.

Has anyone ever asked you a question like that? In my opinion, it's one of the single most damaging kinds of questions one person can ever ask another. A positive, self-affirming response to that question can make people very uncomfortable. It implies that you think you're special, that you are worthy, and that you are capable. Spoiler alert: You are, you are, and YOU ARE! I didn't have the words or the experience to back up my dream back then, but I do now.

The bummer of it all is that I know my friends cared for me and Phil meant nothing by it, but at the time I felt that he was stating how he and the rest of our group truly felt about me. In reality, by buying into his line of questioning, they were revealing how they truly felt about themselves. They revealed themselves in that moment, and once that happens, it's not easy to go back. I'd always loved how open and progressive my group of friends were, but in that moment, I experienced the opposite. My own friends, kids I'd spent years with, could not see potential in me, and that hurt.

Now, I'm not talking the kind of hurt that I've carried with me waiting for the moment to reveal it in a book that I'm writing for humanity, because that would be weird. It hurt me in the way that hurtful things so often do, by planting a seed of doubt that would grow and grow over the years. By itself, the statement held no power, but paired with the years of disappointment in myself that would follow, the words carried more and more weight with each passing failure.

Also, I am 99 percent sure not a single one of my friends even remembers the conversation we had that night, just like I'm sure I've said plenty of stuff to hurt people over the years that I'm not even aware of. This isn't a story about petty friends trying to hurt one another; it's simply an example of words carrying weight. To be fair, I was holding in so much back then that I would dissect every word that was said to me. When you're hiding your true identity, that tends to happen.

Still, the lack of support that night, legitimate or simply perceived, stuck with me.

Every time I had a bad audition or failed to book another job, that thought of "Who do you think you are?" would nudge its way back into the front of my mind and lower my self-belief. Over time, that self-doubt chipped further and further away at me until I was a shell of the confident young man I'd once been. For my own mental health and happiness, I had to course correct that way of thinking. I had to make a decision a few years ago that I would never again live my life according to anyone else's personal beliefs or opinions of me. I once read somewhere that what someone thinks or says about you has everything to do with them and actually nothing to do with you. That sentiment has sustained me through some of the toughest moments in my life and through many ups and downs in Hollywood that I could not have navigated so effectively had I cared what others thought of me.

Also, I know now that their response may have just been a fleeting thought, holding no true value for any of them, even though it held immense value for me, clearly. My high school friends were and are still some of the kindest, most awesome people I've ever known, and I know they were only reacting to the AJ they'd seen in action up to that point. I threw them a curveball and they reacted, but I was being vulnerable and did not like the reaction I got. Their words are on them, my reaction is on me.

I share this story to illustrate a simple point: Words matter, so be very careful and intentional with the words that come out of your mouth. But of equal importance, how we receive words matters, and THAT is what I'd like to focus on. How you perceive words that are being spoken to you or about you can change the course of your day, your week, your month, or even your year. Yes, I just used the theme song from *Friends* to drive home an idea, and you are welcome, because *Friends* is one of the greatest sitcoms of all time!

Seriously though, each of us is in complete control of how we receive messages from the world around us. As a nineteen-year-old boy, I didn't have the capacity to process a few harmless words in a healthy manner, and it has taken me nearly twenty years to go back and look at that night from a different perspective. The shift took me a long time; let's make sure the same can't be said about you.

Is there a story—a false narrative—that you've been telling yourself for so long that you don't know how it even started? While you think about that, I'll go ahead and answer the question for you. YES! Yes is the answer because you are a human, and that's okay. The trick is pinpointing the origin of that damaging self-talk and doing something about it—you can now shift your perspective on a "truth" that may never have been based in any sort of truth at all.

These lies are usually so ingrained in our psyche that we don't even know they exist, and even if we are aware of them, we usually don't have the first idea as to how we should go about correcting them. Luckily for you, my friend, I've corrected a lot of messed up lies that I'd accepted as truth for many years, so I've got some tricks to help you do the same.

Script Rewrites

First, I want you to grab a pen. No pencils allowed; I don't want you regretting anything you're about to write down and then erasing it, because there are no wrong answers. I want you as physically connected to this exercise as possible.

Next, get out your phone and set the alarm for five minutes. Make a mental promise to yourself that in the next five minutes, you are going to be 100 percent transparent and brutally honest with yourself. Once you've made that commitment, not a moment before, then you're ready for the next step. Are you ready? Are you sure? Okay, I believe in you, so here goes.

Start the timer, and for the next five minutes, write down every single thing that anyone has ever told you about yourself that you have accepted as truth that has had any sort of negative impact on your life. I'll wait.

Okay. Great. The hard part is out of the way. Flip the paper over, take a deep breath, and know that just because you wrote those words and they may be stirring up some yucky emotions inside of you right now, that does not mean a single one of them is true. That doesn't mean you might not have written down a few character flaws that may have been pointed out to you by those close to you, because we all have areas of our lives that need to evolve. For this exercise, we're not focusing on those. For this exercise, we're only concerned with the lies you've accepted as truths. Are you ready? Great!

Now, set your alarm again, but this time, give yourself ten seconds. It's important that you stick to this short time frame, and you'll understand why in a moment. Start the timer, flip the paper back over, and circle the one thing on your list that has caused you the most hurt in your life—the one thing that you have accepted as true about yourself but know in your heart just isn't so. You can only circle one, and you only have 10 seconds, so go with your gut on this and don't change your answer. This gets a little tricky, because your psyche will start playing tricks on you right about now.

A few different things could be happening. One, you want to change you answer because you've started to overthink it and you think you should've circled something else. That's a lie. The truth is that your instincts are always right, you've just probably forgotten how to listen to them over the years. You may also be feeling the need to change your answer because your gut tells you that examining the one thing you circled will be uncomfortable, and nobody likes being uncomfortable.

Well, I hope that one word has you squirming right now! If it does, you should be very excited, because you're about to shift your perspective on that word and fall in love with it.

That word or phrase is your new best friend. I want you to write it on paper with hearts around it, I want you to say it out loud to yourself throughout the day, and I want you to fall madly in love with it—AFTER we flip it.

Here's an example. I've done this exercise, so I'll share the phrase I'd accepted as a personal truth but always knew deep down wasn't an accurate description of me, which is why I circled it.

"You're a bullshitter." That was my phrase, and it took me thirty-seven years to rethink it. I come from a family of storytellers, and while there is a fair amount of bullshitting that goes on in my family, I know that I am more than that, so I flipped the narrative on the negative self-talk I'd attached to that specific phrase. So now, whenever that thought creeps back into my mind, I repeat out loud to myself: "AJ, you are intelligent, your words are purposeful, and you have a positive impact on people."

So, whatever your word or phrase may be, I want you to FLIP it, REPEAT it, and OWN it!

CHAPTER SIX:

RATTLED AF

Scene 91: The Perfect Desk Chair.

EXT. ASHLEY FURNITURE — NIGHT

A blur of cars drive past the storefront as we PAN in.

INT. ASHLEY FURNITURE - HOME OFFICES - NIGHT

A PATRON walking by a home office setup stops to admire a pristine desktop. She then turns toward MUFFLED ARGUING with a look of worry on her face. She hurries off.

A few STORE EMPLOYEES also turn toward the arguing, the increased volume of the nearby scuffle grabbing their attention.

We FOLLOW their gaze toward AJ and Emile situated at the side of the room. AJ is sitting in a black desk chair and Emile is looking exhausted.

"We're not getting a black chair; I think they're so tacky and I can't write a book feeling like I'm sitting in a stuffy office somewhere, wasting my life away!"

I was adamant about not wanting a black office chair. I'd spent weeks searching for what I thought I did want, but kept coming up empty handed. Emile was beyond frustrated, but still supporting me on my quest.

"Boo, I can't help you find the perfect desk chair if you don't tell me what it is you're looking for."

"I don't know, Emile. If I knew, we'd have it already. I just know that I don't like anything we've seen yet, but I also know in my gut that when I see it I'll know."

Emile took a deep breath, bit his tongue, and remained supportive. He knew what was really going on, but also knows me well enough to know he had to choose when to call me out on my bullshit. As my first-world stress level reached a fever pitch, he instinctively knew this was not the time.

"Whatever, I'm over it. I'm so sick of looking for this stupid chair and we've just wasted our Friday night at a furniture store. Let's just grab some food and head home."

I'd reached my limit for the day.

So, home we went.

I just couldn't let it go. So, I hopped on my laptop and searched all the same websites I'd visited a million times before, looking for this magical desk chair that would bring me such comfort that I'd have no choice but to write a bestseller. I didn't find it, so we went to bed.

I was feeling overwhelmed by the search; I was anxious that my boyfriend was growing tired of my excuses and, most importantly, I was afraid that if I did actually find the perfect chair that my excuses would no longer be valid. I was afraid of succeeding, so I was self-sabotaging and Emile knew it.

I'm going to be real honest with you: I believe wholeheartedly that I was created to share not only my story, but the stories of people around the world. I have within me the ability to impact positive change in people's lives. We all do. We all have the ability to leave our mark on the world—if we find the courage to do so.

But how could I leave my mark if I didn't have the perfect chair to do it from? I'm an expert at avoidance, at procrastination, and at doing anything on earth that could possibly keep me from achieving what my heart knows is my destiny. It's just a fact. I had convinced myself that without this perfect chair that I knew must exist, I would not be able to write this book that I wasn't 100 percent certain would ever actually exist anywhere other than in my heart.

The desk came easily. Emile and I walked into a furniture store that was going out of business and purchased the beautiful white lacquered desk I'm sitting at right now for only $300 (original price: $800).

Side note: I asked when the store would be closing its doors for good and the salesman nervously responded with, "Five days, I think…yeah, five days." This motivated me to buy the desk without hesitation and I even saved money by agreeing to take it home in the box and put it together myself.

I drove by the same store recently, a few months later and it's still open. I think I was conned, but I love my desk so I'm cool with it.

The irony in this is that I had set out to replace all the Ikea pieces in my home with "adult" furniture, you know, the stuff that comes pre-assembled. Three hours, a double bourbon on the rocks and a lot of back pain later, my desk was complete and I knew I was on my way to a bestselling book!

There was only one problem: I still hadn't found the damn desk chair!

I had in my mind this idea of the perfect chair that I would sit comfortably in for hours on end while I churned out the book of a generation, the book that would connect souls through the shared stories of some of my favorite people. I had spent countless hours reconnecting with any old friend with even an ounce of interior decorating ability, driving to furniture stores in and around LA that I had no idea existed, and researching websites that would put Chip and Joanna Gaines's Pinterest board to shame. (If you don't know who Chip and Joanna Gaines are, Google the pure awesomeness that is this decorating duo from Waco, Texas, or turn on HGTV at any point throughout the day and there's a good chance an episode of their show *Fixer Upper* will be airing. Also, I don't really know if Chip & Joanna even have a Pinterest board, and on the odd chance they find out I mentioned them in this book, I want to clarify that I'm not an expert on their social media habits as they pertain to their interior design empire. Also, I just really want to meet them and I believe in putting dreams out into the universe, so there you have it.)

My search brought us to that frustrating Friday night at an Ashley Furniture in downtown LA, surrounded by black office chairs, where I almost ended my five-year relationship with Emile. He's twenty-eight, I'm not, so we have different tastes when it comes to things like furniture. Mine is exquisite, his is…his. I'm totally sort of

kidding, but only about the personal taste stuff, because this search really did almost tear us apart, at least in my head.

I left Ashley Furniture in downtown LA as they closed that night, convinced that I was, once again, incapable of accomplishing anything because I still couldn't decide on a stupid chair.

Often times, and by "often," I mean "almost always," when I start to feel like a failure I turn inwards. I usually crave some sort of fast food, something like McDonald's because it reminds me of my childhood and then I get quiet and stare off into space. Not many people see this side of me, because I'm the guy from TV that always seems happy and has great hair (seriously though, my hair is great). In actuality, I'm really great at being great for other people. I give the best advice, I'll show up to move furniture at the drop of a dime and I host the best Christmas parties, because those things come easy to me. I love people and even more so, I love making people happy. It breaks my heart whenever I see anyone hurting or feeling unseen or unheard. Nothing gives me greater joy than helping people see their own beautifully unique awesomeness. When it comes to myself though, I always fall short and, as I finished my Big Mac during our ride home, I knew I'd fallen short yet again. I had a stomach ache and still no chair.

The search continued for another week and the pressure only intensified because the following weekend was Labor Day and we all know the best furniture deals of the year can be found during that week. I wish I didn't have to work within a budget, but money management has never really been a strength of mine, so I was determined to find exactly what I had no idea what I was looking for and it was going to be just the right price! Also, "just the right price" means dirt cheap, but fancy looking and super comfortable. Sometimes I set absurdly high expectations and then convince myself that if those expectations aren't met, then it must mean one of two things. First, it could mean that I just haven't tried hard enough. Like, somehow, after all this time of searching for the chair and still not finding it, the solution would be to do more of the same and just sort of hope for a different result. I grew up in a small farming community...I'm not a quitter. (Full transparency, I didn't grow up on a farm, but I have milked a cow and cow milkers don't quit!)

The second option, and the one that's true more often than not, is that my expectations were never realistic and subconsciously set by me to block myself from ever truly reaching my full potential.

"AJ, it's just a chair. Your book will be amazing no matter where you write it. Stop doubting yourself and just start writing."

I knew Emile was right, but this struggle was about so much more than the chair. It was about what the chair represented: the end of a long line of excuses that I'd created to buffer myself from the vulnerability that comes with putting my deepest thoughts, hopes, dreams and fears into words that others can use to judge me. That thought legit terrified me, but not writing the book actually terrified me much more.

So, Labor Day Weekend arrived, we drove to some furniture stores, but decided to head to a friend's pool party for a few hours and enjoy ourselves instead of stewing over this chair of doom. We had a great time, we decompressed, and fully removed ourselves from Chair Gate. However, the next day were met with a harsh reality, one neither of us were quite ready to face. On Monday, the final day of Labor Day furniture sales, we went back to arguing about dumb stuff, scoured the internet for chairs like we'd been doing for weeks, drove back to West Elm for the third time and still found nothing. Finally, as the sun set on that final day of deals and discounts, I thought to myself and then repeated out loud to Emile, "Let's go check out Office Depot." How I'd never thought to check a store that specializes in office supplies for an OFFICE SUPPLY might seem a little dense to some or all of you, but my mind was laser focused on specific stores and websites that I had been referred to, so the Depot was nowhere on my radar.

As we walk in to the store, my best friend, sometimes therapist and pastor, Therese called me on the phone. She knew immediately that I was stressed because she could hear it in my voice. After I explained to her my obnoxious first-world problem, she laughed and calmed me down, like she has a million times before. Then it happened: As I was ready to throw in the towel, I saw it: The most gorgeous white leather office chair was right there in front of me. I literally gasped and thanked my friend for being the positive energy I'd needed in order to find the chair of my writing virginity dreams. And, the icing on the cake: THE CHAIR WAS ON SALE! I thanked my friend profusely, I kissed my boyfriend, I called my mom (because that's what I do every time anything ever happens), and then we drove home, where I then had to put the chair together, piece by piece, Ikea style.

After only thirty minutes or so (I've gotten really good at putting furniture together), the chair of doom had transformed into the chair of our dreams. The leather was soft, the arm rests were perfectly angled and the back was the perfect height for my 6'5" frame. As I stared at the perfect desk chair, a realization came over me like a tsunami. This chair, this perfect desk chair that I'd searched far and wide for, this chair had been there in front of me all along. I'm not speaking metaphorically here, I'd looked up this exact chair no less than fifty times in the past ten days and decided against it, erasing it from my memory each and every time.

When I realized this and then confirmed it by going through the search history on my laptop, I was blown away and almost disgusted with myself. Almost. I had been so focused on all the things that could go wrong if I were to actually find this dream chair and write this book that I was self-sabotaging and literally blind to what was right in front of me all along.

Who can relate?

As I processed this revelation, I was able to show myself some grace and decided that I would dig deeper to find the meaning in this ten-day journey, a meaning that could help me to break through my bad habits and hopefully help you, my friend at home holding this book, to learn something too. The perfect chair existed all along. It was actually right in front of my nose from the moment I decided to start my search, but I simply wasn't ready to see it. My mind was too busy telling me lies about my own ability to find the perfect chair to sit and write my first book and, more importantly, my heart was not showing gratitude for the process that would bring me to the chair I'm sitting in at this very moment. Without gratitude for the journey, I was lost and, truth be told, I've spent most of my life feeling lost, which tells me that I've probably spent most of my life not being grateful for all the countless blessings that I've received. A simple phone call from a special friend shifted my conscious self so quickly, that I was able to see something that had been right in front of me all along.

Script Rewrites

Pick up the phone, call someone you care
about and ask how they're doing and
just listen.

CHAPTER SEVEN:

FUNNY AF

Scene 76: A Shit Show & A Broken Toe

EXT. EL CAPITAN THEATER — EVENING

The streets are busy in front of the theater as a CROWD OF PEOPLE dressed to the nines are entering the main doors of the EL CAPITAN.

The dazzling lights of the sign illuminate the crowd and make the sequins on a multitude of dresses sparkle like twinkling stars.

Cars zoom past the crowd, HONKING their way down the road.

MUFFLED YELLING slowly drowns out the cars.

INT. EL CAPITAN THEATRE — BASEMENT — EVENING

BACKSTAGE WORKERS hustle back and forth as they frantically run around each other.

One WOMAN angrily SLAPS her clipboard.

PRODUCTION ASSISTANT

"Hurry up, people! We're starting in five!"

In the midst of it all is AJ, sitting alone underneath the stairwell with a grin on his face, embracing the absurdity of the moment. His sharp black tuxedo contrasts with the ornery look he projects to the ground.

He'd just been kicked out of his dressing room by Obba Babatundé and his posse.

"So, I guess I'll just sit here until someone comes and gets me," I muttered to myself.

I was about to host my very first awards show at Disney's famous El Capitan Theatre on Hollywood Boulevard with Emmy winner Adrienne Bailon-Houghton, and I'd just been booted from my own dressing room by another Emmy winner. I was obviously the least important person in the equation, so under the stairwell I sat...alone.

It would all go by in a flash, or more like a disastrous explosion, but this night would prove to be one of the greatest nights of my life. I thought I was about to host a two-hour awards ceremony. In reality, I was about to play ringmaster to a five-hour-long, three-ring circus that would become one of my proudest professional achievements. The universe was conspiring to build my confidence and help me write this book, in more ways than one.

As I sat up in my bed the next morning, I asked myself three very specific questions. "How the fuck did I survive last night? Why on earth did they pay me so much money? Is Melanie Griffith's toe okay?"

The night before had been without a doubt the most absurd night of my entire life, and I sort of loved every single minute of it.

Okay, fine, I LOVED EVERY MINUTE OF IT!

I'm sure you're dying to know what made last night so magical for me, but in order to give this story the love it truly deserves, we have to take it all the way back to the Tuesday before...six days prior.

I'd been writing in my own version of a manifestation/gratitude journal for a solid two days, and in true AJ fashion, I had become frustrated with the lack of results by the second day. I'm not the most patient person, especially when I was feeling like I was putting myself out there in an attempt to buy into some ancient mystic voodoo bullshit that I was certain wouldn't work, but inside was desperately hoping would. I've asked God for quite a bit in life. I've probably gotten more of the things I've asked for than I realize, but as of that Tuesday, I was getting specific. So when Wednesday rolled around and I wasn't seeing my deepest hopes and dreams come to fruition, doubt started to creep in. However, this time was different. THIS TIME, I had made up my mind that I would not let something as silly as doubt get in my way. I knew I had to stay strong and was mildly certain I could do it for the long haul, or at least for another few days, maybe even a week. Then, something unthinkable happened.

On Friday, my phone rang.

I'd love to tell you that I picked it up immediately and that in that moment, my manifestation journal came to life, but that's not exactly how it went down. The reality is that I did what I usually do when I don't recognize a phone number. First, I never answer it because I'm sure it's someone politely trying to remind me that I'm behind on some random bill I've tried desperately to avoid or just altogether forget. Then, I stare at my iPhone hoping and praying that whoever was calling me had the courtesy to leave a voicemail, even though I'm the asshole who didn't even answer the phone in the first place. The worst possible scenario is that they don't leave a message and I'm left agonizing over who the call could've been from the rest of the week.

Was that someone calling to tell me I'd just won the lottery? That would be completely illogical, considering that I've never bought a ticket. I never said my thoughts are in any way rational.

Had I just missed a call from a casting director reaching out to tell me he or she would like to make me into the next Ryan Seacrest? That's a call I'd hate to miss.

Well, in this story, I watched the phone ring and ring and ring. Then I waited, and I waited, and I waited. It felt like an eternity even though I had no idea what I was waiting for. And then it happened. That red dot showed up, and I knew I had a voicemail. My life was about to change forever!

Well, that might be a bit of a dramatic overreaction to a simple voicemail, but when I called back and got the news that I wasn't ready to receive three minutes earlier, I felt a sudden rush of joy accompanied by a tinge of frustration with myself for not having had the nerve to answer the phone in the first place. But here I was, and I was receiving the news, and it was good…so good!

On the other end of the call was a woman with a lot of energy. I couldn't quite pinpoint her accent, but I was able to decipher about half of her words and filled in the rest from there. I clearly heard her say things like, "I'm a huge fan of yours" and, "I can only pay you $5,000," so maybe her English wasn't quite as poor as I am pretending it was. Also, I'm fluent in only one language, so who am I to judge?

Regardless, she wanted to hire me for a job and pay me $5,000! Full transparency, up until that point I'd never made that much money in a single day in my entire life, so without hesitation, I made up my mind to accept whatever job she'd just described to me in broken English. Then, I did what you're supposed to do in this city, I asked her to reach out to my talent manager to handle the details, which she agreed to do. So I called him immediately to tell him I'd just been offered a king's ransom to do something and that it was his job to figure out what I'd just agreed to. "Yes" was the answer, I just needed him to figure out what the question was.

So, this mystery woman called my manager Glen, and they had a frantic chat, which he then relayed to me. It turned out she needed me to host an awards show, the CineFashion Film Awards at the El Capitan Theatre on Hollywood Boulevard. I'd never heard of it, but I didn't care! Barbra Streisand was set to attend along with some other notable guests, and I was to be the emcee of the evening, along with Adrienne Bailon-Houghton.

I WAS PUMPED!

Immediately, I started running through every single Barbra Streisand reference I could think of, asking myself if I should call her Babs, Barbra, or Miss Streisand. Maybe she preferred just being called GOAT (Greatest of All Time), or maybe she'd prefer I not acknowledge her at all. I had so many *Funny Girl* and *A Star Is Born* stories ready to share with her and wanted to make the most of this rare opportunity. In my head, our souls would connect during my opening monologue, during which I would explain how many times my mom and I had watched *A Star Is Born* together over the years (mostly because I'm pretty sure my mom had a crush on Kris Kristofferson), but the "Ha ha, I was a little gay boy from Ohio" moment would come when I revealed that I've always been more of a *Funny Girl* kinda guy myself. We would bond immediately and become instant best friends for all eternity!

Well, that's how it all went in my head.

The afternoon of the show I was abnormally calm. I hadn't slept that well the night before, so maybe I was just feeling subdued, but I definitely wasn't anxious. I'd prepared for this moment my entire life and knew that I was ready. I was definitely nervous to meet Babs (I'd settled on that overnight), but not nervous about doing it in front of a theater full of onlookers. Then, the unthinkable happened. The entire lineup of A-list celebrities I'd been told a mere twenty-four hours before would be attending had changed, and you guessed it, no Babs. I felt deflated. I felt embarrassed. And for the first time, I felt anxious.

When I'd had a vision in my head of how the night would unfold, I had felt prepared. Now that I had no clue what to expect, I was moderately terrified. I facetimed my mom, because this wasn't the sort of earth-shattering news you should share via text or even a phone call. I needed her to see my face and see how badly I was hurting. Actually, I probably just needed to see her face so that I could calm down and get back into the right headspace. Either way,

Babs would not be seeing my opening monologue (or anything else of me for that matter).

You know who would be in the audience for my opening monologue? Stevie Wonder, Melanie Griffith, Donna Karan, Dionne Warwick, Akon, and a bunch of other talented people whom I admire. Also, Tara Reid. For the life of me, I still can't figure out how she got her amputated hand back in *Sharknado 4: The Fourth Awakens*, but I digress.

I would be doing what I love, next to a talented co-host in front of a roomful of icons, and getting paid to do so, with or without my favorite "Funny Girl" in the audience. This was a blessing, and I was prepared for the opportunity!

I was also just days away from heading home to start writing this book and had about $2.47 to my name, so the timing of this payday could not have been more perfect; my manifestation journal was working!

God is good, all the time!

So as I waited under that stairwell for the show to begin, a sense of calm came over me. Nothing had gone as expected, yet here I was about to host my first awards show alongside an Emmy winner.

Moments later, we were whisked backstage as the opening number commenced. Obba did a full-on Ziegfeld Follies-styled song and dance routine, surrounded by a supporting cast of female dancers in gorgeous costumes. He had the audience on the edge of their seats and ready to have a good time.

"Adrienne, AJ...you're up!"

My heart was about to beat out of my chest. The moment those stage lights hit me as I saw the packed house for the first time, I knew that I belonged.

I was home.

Our opening monologue went off without a hitch, and we were finding our rhythm. I'd never worked with Adrienne before, but learned very quickly why she's an Emmy winner. She was an absolute pro. Also, she wore the most gorgeous sequined burgundy dress, and I'd happened to pack a burgundy velvet bow tie to wear with my tux that matched her dress perfectly, so the universe was clearly conspiring to make us look like we'd planned this fashion moment.

As we walked backstage, having just nailed our opening, the first presenter of the night handed out an award and we were escorted by the stage manager to the location of our next shot, in the audience. As we stood in the aisleway among the audience, we introduced the next video package—and it never started rolling. We stood smiling and waited for what felt like an eternity.

Still nothing.

To our left were Dionne Warwick and Stevie Wonder; to our right, my boyfriend Emile and our friends Therese and Drew. I'd wanted a support system in the audience, and they were given great seats for what I thought would be my first, flawless turn at hosting an awards show.

They were about to get a show, all right!

The video took forever to start, and when it finally did, there was no audio. The stage manager panicked and asked us to start talking again.

"Adrienne, AJ...we need you two to vamp now," we heard in our earpieces.

"So, Adrienne, what a fun show, right?"

"Yeah, AJ, I loved that opening number, and the fashion tonight is so impressive!"

What we thought would be a quick distraction from the technical difficulties taking place behind the scenes turned into fifteen minutes of vamping that turned into a comedy set. Adrienne is a well-established musician and Emmy winner; she didn't need to prove anything to anyone and was more than happy to let me take the lead. So I did! I started rambling on about the guests in the audience and how excited I was to be hosting the show with such a talented co-host, and then at one point, I started running out of material. Fifteen minutes is a LONG time to be standing in front of an audience with nothing prepared. So I did what I've done my entire life—I started telling stories.

"Are you all having fun? I hope you don't mind the view of my backside. I've got to keep facing forward in case our stage manager says we're ready to go and that little red light on our camera comes back on. I've been working out a lot lately, and I've been doing a lot of squats, so your view should be pretty good right now. How does my butt look?"

WHAT?!? Why on earth was I now talking about my butt and asking an entire theater full of celebrities to stare at it? I'd clearly lost my mind, but once I start rolling there's not much that can stop me.

It's a blessing and a curse.

Notice neither Adrienne nor myself looking at the teleprompter. I was probably talking about my butt.

Adrienne just looked up at me and laughed. She knew better than to jump in and was clearly enjoying the moment. I now had officially gone full-on diarrhea of the mouth, and there was no end in sight. I was waiting for our stage manager, the executive producer, or God to speak into my earpiece and tell me I could stop talking, but that never happened. I rambled on and on about nothing in particular and at one point glanced over and saw Dionne Warwick and Stevie Wonder just giggling at me.

"I'm a train wreck, Miss Warwick, aren't I? Trust me, I'm laughing on the inside too...under the internal tears."

She laughed and told me I was great!

What?!? How could she think I was doing great? I was single-handedly tanking the entire show and knew I'd never be hired for anything ever again. It's hard to describe the feeling of being left alone to entertain an entire theater of celebrities and their guests with zero notice. I'd never been in a situation quite like this before, and it was unnerving, but also kind of amazing. I was sure my career would be over after that night, so I was making that most of it and having a blast in the process!

The entire stage went pitch-black for a good portion of my vamp/comedy set.

The show was total chaos. As it turns out, someone from Stevie Wonder's team had plugged something in backstage where it wasn't supposed to be plugged in, and it had shorted the circuit board. And, no, it wasn't Stevie who did the plugging, although that would've been brilliant, you know, because he's blind (I told you I have a sick sense of humor)!

In the moment, I was just trying to keep up with the rapidly changing dynamics of the evening.

At one point, the director simply took off her headset and said she had a flight to catch. She was a pretty awful woman so I think her absence actually helped the show. My hope is that she flew to a remote beach location somewhere tropical and drank herself into a stupor. She was crazy mean, and if I were her, I know I would've needed a drink, God bless her.

Eventually, the power came back on, and the show resumed without its director. Each time it felt like we were getting into a rhythm, something new would fall apart, and we were again left to trying to glue the show back together. About midway through the evening, Melanie Griffith was to receive an award of some sort, and Adrienne and I would be introducing the segment from the audience (or the house, as it's technically called). We were legit sitting on a large speaker placed on the side of the theater because our producer had no direction as where to place us, because our DIRECTOR had "peaced out"!

Luckily, this was being recorded and not airing live. As messy as the production felt, it could all be pieced together later by editors, and through the magic of Hollywood, the finished product would be amazing (and it was).

The producer was a bundle of nerves, and the next couple of minutes were about to become one of the funniest things I've ever experienced.

"Adrienne, AJ, it's almost time to introduce the next portion of the show. Please stand by."

Like we had a choice.

Then, I heard our producer say, "Yes, I've got eyes on Melanie. GO!"

He then turned to me, and as the announcer welcomed "Academy Award nominee and Golden Globe winner Melanie Griffith" to the stage, he said, "AJ, that's Melanie Griffith right there, isn't it?"

He was pointing to a random woman sitting in the audience who was at least eighty years old. This was not good.

"I'm sorry. What? Her? No, that's definitely not Melanie Griffith. I think that's just some lady." I couldn't believe this was happening, but I was trying to stop another train wreck from happening, because I knew I'd have to do the damage control and I was fresh out of material.

It was too late. The announcer had already welcomed her to the stage, but that poor woman just sat there, completely unaware of the chaos taking place around her. Also, SHE WASN'T MELANIE GRIFFITH, so that seat was exactly where she belonged. Adrienne and I looked at each other and just started laughing. This was comedy gold!

As the audience waited patiently and a soft murmur filled the theater, the announcer tried a couple more times to lure Melanie to the stage. There was one major problem: Melanie Griffith, everyone's favorite "working girl," had left the building!

Also, if you haven't seen *Working Girl* yet, do yourself a favor and check it out. She's spectacular!

So once again, we were asked to vamp as production assistants scrambled to locate their lost star.

Adrienne wasn't having it.

That poor woman had been pulled in every direction the entire night, circling that theater multiple times, because without a director, we were flying blind! At one point we were walked outside into the alley to cross the theater because no one knew how to get us where we needed to be while remaining indoors—and this happened at least five times. The alleyway around and behind the El Capitan Theatre is hilly, uneven, and full of gravel and shards of broken glass. She was wearing a ball gown and high heels. We were both being reminded of the importance of a director.

So, I went to work once again, cracking jokes about our missing celeb. It felt like I was bombing. The truth was that I was getting exactly what I'd prayed for earlier that day and a million times before.

Every time I've been given the opportunity to do what I love, I pray for God to use me to spread joy, to give me the words to impact people's lives, and to show my talents to the people who can give me opportunities to change my life for the better. I didn't realize it in the chaos of the moment, but I was getting exactly what I'd asked for.

Eventually, someone was sent out on stage to accept the award on behalf of Melanie, and it was explained that Miss Griffith had broken her toe during the show and had left to have a doctor look at it. I was told by producers working on the show that she'd actually grown frustrated by all the delays and had decided to bounce. I don't know what really happened, but I hope she wasn't bored by my stand-up routine, and I also hope she didn't actually break her toe.

Side note: If she didn't break her toe (and I'm 99 percent sure she didn't), what a weird and random excuse to make up for her absence. It was a rather absurd night all around, so this was really par for the course, all things considered.

Eventually, we made it to the end of the show. What was supposed to be a two, maybe three-hour gig was now heading into hour five. Needless to say, the audience was getting restless. Stevie Wonder had performed (three times, because there had been an issue with his audio the first two times), Donna Karan had given an impassioned speech after being honored for her philanthropic work in Haiti, and Forest Whitaker was honored as well, except he was filming a movie in Africa or doing philanthropic work and couldn't make it to the show. I hate when that happens at awards shows—first Barbra, and now Forest.

I am grateful they managed to fix Stevie's audio issues, because seeing him perform up close like that was a rare pleasure. He'd performed during the holidays a couple of years back while I was working as the entertainment anchor on *Good Day LA*, and it doesn't matter how many times I see him live, he's a legend and an all-time great!

In addition to performing, he was also presenting Dionne Warwick with an award that evening. Ironically, his entire speech was on the teleprompter. As at most awards shows, the teleprompter was a large TV in the back of the audience from which those on stage, myself included, read their script lines. It's lined up in a way that makes it look as if we're looking directly into the camera when we're actually looking just above or below it. I'm not really sure why they thought a blind man needed a teleprompter, but it was fun to follow along with his words as he gave his beautiful introductory speech...TWICE!

This all-time great not only had to perform three times due to audio issues, something had gone wrong during his first heartfelt speech, so he was asked to return to the stage and introduce the same award again by giving the exact same speech! The coolest part was that he nailed every word once again! He'd had to memorize the entire minutes-long speech and didn't miss a beat. I guess the teleprompter was there so that we could all compare his actual words to his prepared words and be blown away by his precision. He really is an ICON!

Mr. Wonder (that sounds awesome, BTW) was one of the last presenters of the evening, which brought us to the In Memoriam portion of the show. This is always a difficult part of any awards show to watch, let alone introduce, as talented artists who've passed away in the year prior are honored. The moment needed to be handled with grace and dignity.

"Wow, what a legend! What a party tonight has been! What a great day to be alive and to be here in this iconic theater, sharing this moment with all of you!"

"Yeah, AJ, let's keep the party going!" Adrienne was hanging in there like the pro that she is, and we were genuinely in this thing together, no matter how many times the wheels had fallen off.

That first part was ad-libbed by each of us.

"And now, it's time to honor those we've lost!"

This part was not.

Why was I reading this first line in the teleprompter like I was excited to talk about a bunch of dead people? Oh, yeah, BECAUSE OUR DIRECTOR HAD WALKED OUT AND WE WERE FLYING BLIND!

We had no idea what we were about to introduce.

I sounded like a complete asshole, and I knew it. We walked out onto the stage to what sounded like Latin salsa music, which was clearly way too up-tempo for this part of the show. A director would've caught that.

"I'm sorry, nope, I'm not going to say it that way. Can we do that again please?"

I glanced over at Adrienne, and my face clearly read, "WTF," because she looked up at me and nodded in agreement. That was no way to introduce an "In Memoriam" package.

We were on stage in front of a dwindling audience, since a lot of people had grown tired of the delays and decided to "peace out" after one of Stevie's three performances. A younger, less established AJ never would've had the guts to speak up, but this evening had battle-tested me, and I knew it was the right call.

So we marched backstage and waited, and once they began playing more somber music, we walked back onto that stage with reverence for those lost. The audience wasn't feeling it.

They were irritated and leaving in droves by this point. The stage manager stood to our side, just off camera, waving his hands in the air and imploring everyone to take their seats.

"Everyone, please remain seated. I know it's been a long night, but just a few more minutes please," he yelled.

I glanced out into the audience, where Emile and my friends were still solidly in my corner, though laughing hysterically, and it took everything in me not to burst into laughter myself as I continued to read my script in front of an audience that could not have cared less.

"Let's take a moment to honor those we've lost."

As the package ran while I was standing on the stage, the lights of which were lowered, I giggled to myself, thinking, "Well, does this include the hundreds of audience members we've lost as this show has dragged on? How about Melanie, are we honoring her right now, because no one knows where the fuck she is? Also, I wonder how her toe's doing?"

On the outside, I was stoic. Remembering the paycheck that had already been handed to me and was now resting safely in my breast pocket was all the motivation I needed to remain professional. And all those people were dead, so I didn't want to be the jerk who was laughing during their tribute. If the audience only knew all that had actually gone down during the course of that show!

Finally, after five hours, we concluded the show. Adrienne and I hugged, knowing we'd both experienced something only we would ever truly understand, and she was escorted to her car. Emile and our friend Drew were waiting for me at the side of the stage, ready to give me a big congratulatory hug. Therese had left thirty minutes before, because it was close to midnight and she had to work the next morning. We'd had no idea we'd be there this late!

My friends looked at me with an expression that just read, "WTF was that!" They also gave me a round of applause, knowing how hard I'd just worked and how stressful the night must've been for me. They each work on camera as well, so there was an understanding of what I'd just gone through. They gushed about the way I'd handled myself and kept the show on track, and I was so grateful for their words. I'd asked for God to use me to spread joy, and I could tell by the audience's reactions and the feeling in my heart that I'd done that.

I had also asked Him to give me an opportunity to show my talents to the people who could give me opportunities to change my life for the better. Prayers like this usually take a little more time.

But then, something incredible happened.

I looked down at my phone.

To: Rika

Sun, Oct 8, 9:27 PM

That was insane

Squats!!!!!!

Sitting next to someone who said AJ is the new Dick Clark

OMG you just made my day! He was my idol as a little kid 🙈

!!! Are you surviving over there?

OMG you know where I am?!?

I was in the audience

Shut up!!!

I know exactly what you've been up to

Squats!!!! LOL

So you've seen me dying a slow painful death all night!!!

You did good

The God is Good was my best

Such a great learning experience...always grateful for an opportunity to grow lol

Lol

Mon, Oct 9, 9:12 AM

Sorry I didn't get to see you last night, but your kind words meant so much to me in the midst of a chaotic experience. Thanks for always supporting & encouraging me. Also, Asi's packages were the highlight of the show. 💋

Delivered

Rika, one of my executive producers from all the red carpets I've hosted for Dick Clark Productions over the years, had texted me that earlier in the show, while I was giving one of my off-the-cuff monologues. I hadn't looked at my phone and I'd had no idea she was in the audience, but she had been, and my prayer had been answered. All of the doubt and second-guessing I'd done that entire night disappeared in that moment, and I knew that everything had gone according to plan...His plan.

Being mentioned in the same sentence as one of my idols, Dick Clark, by someone who works for his production company meant and still means so much to me. The night definitely had not gone as planned, but if it had, I wouldn't have had the opportunity to show how I handle chaos, and my personality certainly wouldn't have been on full display. What do you think the likelihood is that someone would've written a joke about my butt looking great from squats? I'm going to guess somewhere close to zero percent. I didn't get what I wanted, but I did get what I asked for, and more importantly, I got what I needed. I was given the opportunity to push beyond my comfort zone and showcase my personality, and it was accompanied by a nice paycheck; not a bad day's work as far as I'm concerned. I had money to put in my bank account so that I could now head home and start writing my book without stressing about debt and bills and all of those things that keep us all from living our best lives.

Everything was falling into place and I was grateful.

I just hope Melanie's toe is okay.

Script Rewrites

How often have you hoped for one outcome in life and received a totally different one? It's easy to try to force situations or manipulate results when we feel uncertain or out of control, but trust me when I say that is a battle you cannot win. You may be able to avoid or delay an outcome from time to time, but what's meant to be will be, so it's our job to learn to embrace the chaos and allow it to build us. There are lessons in every situation; it's up to us to find them.

For this exercise, just think about a moment in your life when something didn't turn out as planned, but ended up resulting in something positive. There's nothing to write down here. Just simply acknowledge that moment, show gratitude for it and ask for more positive unexpected outcomes in the future. Say out loud, "I am grateful for…" followed by the moment you've decided on. For instance, I would say something like, "I am grateful for the opportunity to show how quickly I'm able to think on my feet in front of an audience of my peers!"

You should smile while you do this; I find that smiling helps.

CHAPTER EIGHT:

INTROSPECTIVE AF

Scene 81: AJ Goes on a Sixteen-Day Writing Sabbatical

EXT. AIRPLANE — DAY

A large airliner glides through a blue sky hovering just above the cloud line.

The unrestrained rays of the sun make the airplane gleam brightly.

INT. AIRPLANE - DAY

An ATTENDANT hands down a drink to a PASSENGER. The passenger nods gratefully as the attendant pulls her trolley down the center aisle of the plane.

A BABY CRIES over the LOUD ENGINE of the airplane.

The attendant reaches the next row.

As she smiles down at the next row, she leans down to the MAN in the aisle seat.

ATTENDANT

Anything to drink, sir?

We PAN across the row to AJ who is crammed in the window seat; legs scrunched up practically to his chest.

He is staring out the window of the plane, lost in thought.

"I'll have another Bloody Mary, please."

Three hours into my four-hour flight home and I was on drink number three. My writing sabbatical had officially begun and I was already failing. Awesome. Also, I was borderline drunk and had $24 less in my bank account than when I'd gotten on the plane so, needless to say, the trip had not started out like I'd hoped.

Truth be told, I was a bundle of nerves, and vodka seemed like the most logical way to calm down. It wasn't the worst plan, but it also wasn't helping get me any closer to my goal, which was to go home, write this book, and turn my life around. As I stared into my plastic cup, now holding only ice cubes tinted slightly red, the only thing I wanted to turn around was that plane. I was in over my head and I knew it.

Who on earth was I to be going home on something called a "sabbatical" to write a book?

In my mind, I would use this time in Ohio to reconnect with my roots and find the pathway to the book that's been buried deep inside of me for all these years. This trip would change everything, if I could just ignore the negative self-talk and do what I set out to do!

In my mind, I had visions of a sixteen-day writing sabbatical, mostly because that word conjures up images of wise men on long journeys to enlightenment that lead to deep, meaningful discovery. If you've ever read The Alchemist, then you'll understand what I mean when I say that, in my head, I was Santiago and Celina, Ohio was my Spain. I'd journeyed through the world, learned all I could learn and was ready to return home, full of purpose and ready to write. This would be the pivotal moment in my life I'd searched for since I was a teenager. I was a grown ass man and this was the most adult thing I had ever done. This was my writing sabbatical.

The word feels so romantic, so intelligent, so aspirational. I'd never known any authors growing up, so all I knew of the process I'd either seen in films or imagined in my mind. Just the word author felt so intimidating to me, so I thought I had to kick off my book writing experience in some grand way. I saw myself sitting at the desk of my dead grandmother on the anniversary of her passing, or her birthday (they're only one day apart) and receiving her divine intervention. Her spirit would guide my fingers as they created a masterpiece on the keyboard of my barely functioning MacBook Pro. It's seven years old, slow as molasses, and has a cracked screen. I almost let that convince me that I couldn't write this book. My mind is sneaky and self-doubt is a powerful thing, but I'm more powerful and, once again, my purpose is greater than my fear and my purpose is PEOPLE.

I would sit at my grandma's desk at some point, because why not, but her love and guidance do not lie within that desk. She's in my heart and in my mind. I've delayed so many decisions and avoided so many journeys in my life because the timing didn't feel right or because I didn't feel capable.

I received an internship to Disneyworld in college, but backed out at the last minute because I didn't know if I'd be able to survive so far from home for three months. While living in New York in my mid-twenties, I had the opportunity to work on a six-month contract with a cruise line, traveling the world and making more money than I'd ever made, but backed out at the last minute because I was afraid to be away from my family for that long. The question "who am I to do this new thing" has kept me small for far too long and at 6'5" trust me, that's an impressive feat.

After landing in Ohio, sobering up and arriving home with fire in my heart, I walked out to my parent's sunroom, where my dead grandma's desk now lived.

You're going to learn all about my Grandma Corky in a bit, so you should be excited about that. For now, just know that she's dead.

As I marched into that sunroom, overlooking our pool and the beautiful lake in our back yard, I had my barely working MacBook

Pro in one hand and a cup of coffee in the other. I was even drinking out of a mug I'd bought dead grandma once during a trip to Knott's Berry Farms in Southern California. She had memories of going there as a child, so I thought I'd give her a small piece of her childhood as her life drew to a close. Corky was dead, but her mug and her desk lived on.

The mug was exactly as I'd remembered; the desk however seemed much smaller. Also, I'm larger than I used to be, so sitting at her tiny wooden desk probably wouldn't make all that much sense. I spent my childhood sitting at that desk or hiding under it during intense hours long rounds of hide-and-seek with my cousins, but that AJ was much, much smaller. Regardless, I had a goal and this tiny hurdle would not derail me.

The problem with playing it small is that in doing so, no one benefits. Not me, not my book, not my readers and not the legacy of my dead Grandma Corky, may she rest in peace.

DEAD!

I knew the second I stepped up to that desk for the first time as an adult and with a clear intention, that there was no way I would ever write a single word at it. My mom, sweet as can be, had even organized it and bought a desk lamp to help set the scene for my sixteen days of artistic expression, but in a single moment that all went out the window. Once again, life was teaching me a lesson.

There was no way this was the glamorous piece of fine craftsmanship I'd remembered my grandma sitting at during my childhood. I used to climb under her feet and hide from my sister Kari as our grandma plucked away at her typewriter or penned handwritten notes on birthday cards. She always kept a drawer full of cards for any occasion and her calendar was marked up with birthday and anniversary reminders for every month of the year. That desk was an integral part of my childhood, but there was no way that THIS was THAT desk.

I looked at my mom and we just started to laugh! The best-laid plans rarely play out the way we expect. My memory had failed me and I know dead grandma was laughing right along with us.

I had such specific intentions for this trip home and that moment could have derailed the entire thing, but I was determined not to let that happen. Old AJ may have used it as a silly excuse to give up completely, but new AJ had a good laugh about it and came up with another plan, because new AJ understood that this book is not about him. This book is his love letter to humanity, so quitting this was not an option. Life had placed another roadblock in my path, but I was determined to start writing.

On the opposite side of my parents' sunroom: an oversized chair with an ottoman. THAT is where my sabbatical would begin.

Script Rewrites

I want you to make two lists. First, write down the two or three happiest moments of your entire life. Allow yourself as much time as you need to recall memories that make your heart smile. Once you're happy with your list, I want you to write down the two or three saddest moments of your life. I'm purposely not making any suggestions about the types of memories that should go in either category, because your feelings are yours and they are valid, regardless of how anyone else may view them. I make jokes about my dead grandma, I'm in no position to judge!

Next, I'd like for you to look at both lists with as little emotional attachment as possible. Try not to view any of the memories you wrote down as being either good or bad, but simply as memories. For the sake of this exercise, these are moments in your life that you simply experienced.

Now, I want you to write down the common threads in each of these experiences. Does your list seem family oriented? Is one person prevalent on your list? Does your job tend to be a common theme? Is love the thing that tends to bring you both intense joy and deep sorrow? Does your entire list revolve around your children? Your parents? You?

Whatever your conclusion, if you're being 100 percent honest with yourself, THIS is the thing that makes you tick, but it may also be a huge roadblock for you. That's ok. There is no wrong answer. Hold onto that thing as you continue reading this book and allow it to take you on this journey with me, because it's that thing that that will reveal the pathway to your personal version of true happiness. I'm excited for you! Why, because YOU are what makes me tick!

CHAPTER NINE:

DEAD AF

Scene 49: Grandma

INT. FUNERAL HOME — DAY

There is a gathering of PEOPLE sitting in
a crowded viewing room; all of them facing
the hundreds of brightly colored flowers
surrounding a single casket.

In the casket lies CORKY, now deceased. Her
face is peaceful as her gray curly hair puffs
around her bony cheeks like a frame around
a portrait.

By her side, standing at a podium, is her
grandson, AJ.

With tears in his eyes, he looks over
the crowd.

Many of the guests CRY as they pat their eyes
with handkerchiefs.

Some blot the tears on their wet cheeks with
a sleeve.

AJ fumbles with his suit jacket buttons with
shaky hands.

"Our grandma really was the coolest lady. We all had our own special bond with her, but for Kari and me, she was like a second mother. We were so lucky to have her in our lives for so many years, and as much as I already miss her, I am kind of excited to finally cast a vote for Hillary Clinton that she can't cancel out. Sorry, Grandma, there's nothing you can do about it now!"

The mood shifted as everyone started to chuckle. It was all a blur to me—the phone call letting me know she'd passed, the flight home to Ohio, and this moment in particular. I'd always sort of expected that I'd one day give my grandma's eulogy, but I'd never prepared for it—and now she was dead.

"Our grandma Corky did so many awesome things during her lifetime. Now she's DEAD!"

Most of the people sitting in the room that morning went silent, probably trying to figure out if they'd heard me correctly; not because they were shocked that Corky was dead, since that was pretty obvious, but because they were trying to figure out if I'd really just cracked a joke about my dead grandma WHILE GIVING HER EULOGY.

I totally did.

My cousins and I got the joke, and I'm pretty sure our parents did, too, and that was all that mattered. In the days leading up to her funeral, we had cried so much that we were really just sick of being sad and knew our grandma wouldn't want us to say goodbye to her in that way, so I flipped the script on her eulogy.

"She really was the best! Remember how she used to bake those peanut butter cookies with the Hershey's Kiss on top? She was soooo good at making those...and then she DIED!"

We definitely have a sick sense of humor, but humor is what got us through such a tremendous loss. My cousins are like siblings to me, and having them to lean on during the greatest loss I'd ever known gave me the strength to crack dead grandma jokes and to mention Hillary. My grandma hated her with a passion! We used to send each other emails all the time leading up to the 2008 primary election that would usually go something like this.

"Grandma, just because you found a website that says Hillary is having a lesbian affair with an alien who owns a Nazi bakery where puppies are being made into stew does not mean it's true."

"Well, honey, I just don't trust her," she'd say.

"Okay. Is there something SPECIFIC that you don't trust, Grandma?"

"She lies and I know it!"

These conversations were really partially fun and partially mind-numbing, but mostly we just liked getting under each other's skin a bit. My grandma could more than hold her own, even if she didn't have the most well-thought-out arguments.

"Okay, what exactly did she lie about, Grandma? Maybe if you can tell me that, we can do some research and see if what you believe is actually true or not."

"I don't know, she's just a liar!"

"Okay, Grandma, fair enough. Are there things about her policy positions that bother you? Because I know you pretty well, and I think if you just knew her voting record on a few things that I know are important to you, you might change your mind."

There was a time when logic and appealing to her sensibilities was a surefire way to find common ground. This was not one of those times.

"She's just a bitch!"

Yikes!

"Okay, Grandma, that seems a little harsh, but I'm gonna let you have that one. I'm really not sure what I could even say at this point. Also, could you send me your oyster stuffing recipe for Thanksgiving? You emailed it to me years ago, but I can't seem to find it anywhere."

"Well, honey, I don't really use a recipe for that, but let me see if I can remember how to make it. I know you're going to need oysters... and lots of saltine crackers. I'll email it to you when I get around to it."

"Thanks, Grandma! Hillary 2008! Love, Poofenwaffer!" That was her nickname for me. I have no idea where it came from, but she'd called me that for as long as I could remember. My sister Kari was her Sweet Patootie. I clearly got the better of the two nicknames.

"She's a BITCH! Love, Granny C!" That was my nickname for her. I think that one's pretty self-explanatory.

My grandma was without a doubt the best woman I've ever known. Out of those closest to me, she is the one person in my life with whom I never really had a beef. I don't have mixed emotions about her, and I've never felt the need to speak with a therapist about her. While my relationships with others felt more like a roadblock at times, my relationship with her always made me feel like I could be or do anything.

Giving her eulogy was a rock bottom moment for me, but one I was determined to turn around.

I remember this one time when as a child of maybe seven or eight, I wanted so desperately to be a contestant on *The Bozo Show*! I didn't quite know how I was going to get all the way to Chicago for a taping, but it was a dream of mine that I was not willing to give up. My grandma saw how important this was to me.

We watched *The Bozo Show* each morning as I ate my breakfast on her living room floor. Her living room had been a bedroom when my mom and her siblings had grown up in the house but had later been converted into a small second living room for my grandma, because Grandpa had claimed the main living room for himself. Their house was humble, with only a small single bathroom, but it was perfect. She made me Cinnamon Toast Crunch or a toasted bagel with butter and cream cheese, because everything tastes better with butter. On rare occasions, she even poured me a bowl of Banana Nut Crunch, but that was the expensive stuff, so it didn't happen often. To this day, it's still my favorite cereal and the first thing I look for at the grocery when I'm missing my grandma.

I watched kids compete for prizes being handed out by Bozo and his partner in crime, Cookie. I was never too interested in Cookie, he creeped me the fuck out. But Bozo, he was a star!

Unfortunately, he was also four hours away, which might as well have been forty hours, since I was just a kid with no way of getting to his show. So, my grandma did what she did best.

One morning, after I walked two doors down to her house, she told me she had a surprise out back for me. We walked through the house and out the sliding glass doors, where we exited her living room onto the back patio.

And there in front of me was something I'll never forget.

My grandma had gone into her basement and found five old plastic pails that we used to take to the beach each summer in Michigan. She'd nailed them to a two-by-four, with each bucket about a foot apart in a perfect row. My grandma had recreated "The Grand Prize Game" from *The Bozo Show*!

Back then I pronounced it "The Gwan Pweyes Game" because I had a speech impediment that was really a lot of fun. Kari still says I was the cutest kid because I talked like the Welch's grape juice boy. Personally, I just remember going to speech therapy every week to learn how to properly pronounce the letters "S" and "R." Who knew that someday I would make a living off of my voice. Just another way that God uses our struggles to create opportunities, I guess.

In this particular moment, God had used my grandma to make my dream come true!

I couldn't contain myself, and as I type this story, I can't help but tear up while remembering how perfect that day was and how loved I felt in that moment. She handed me a ping-pong ball and told me to step up to the line, which was a piece of masking tape on her patio. Then she pulled out a Fisher Price microphone that Kari had previously been given for her birthday.

"Ladies and gentlemen, boys and girls, it's time for the GRAND PRIZE GAME! And playing today, we have Joe Blow from Kokomo!"

I had no idea where Kokomo was, but it sounded exotic and the whole thing rhymed, so I was sold!

Kari and me coloring on grandma's back patio as kids, the same patio that would act as the "studio" for *The Bozo Show*. I was apparently very excited about coloring books.

With each shot I made, she had a small prize waiting for me. With each success, the anticipation grew, and while I can't remember what the grand prize was that day, I do remember how she made me feel, and that was more special than any prize. It's memories like this one that gave me the strength to speak in front of her loved ones as she lay peacefully next to me in a casket, DEAD!

I wrapped up what felt like a rambling, incoherent mess of a eulogy with some sweet words about the impact she'd had on all of our lives and how grateful I was that I'd found the courage to reveal the real me to her before she'd passed. I never came out to my grandpa, who'd died years before, and had never fully recovered from that. With some unwanted help from my mom, I had come out to my grandma a couple of years earlier, and it had taken our relationship to a place it had never been.

I remember the night my mom told me that grandma knew I was gay like it happened yesterday.

"Honey, your grandma knows you're gay. I think you should call her."

I was living in Columbus, Ohio at the time, twenty-five and about to graduate from college.

"What?!? Mom, what do you mean she knows I'm gay?"

"Honey, I knew you'd be upset, but she was asking why you never brought home any girls, and it just sort of came out. We had a good talk about it, and she's fine, but I think she should hear it from you. Your grandma loves you very much, it'll be fine."

This was a conversation I was NOT ready to have with my grandma, but one I'd regretted not having the courage to have with my grandpa, so I knew this was a blessing in disguise. That still didn't mean it was a blessing I was ready to receive.

"Oh my God, mom, how does my sexuality just casually come up in conversation? I don't think I'm ready to talk to her about this yet."

Truth be told, I would never have been "ready" to have this conversation with my grandma, even though I needed to. I'd come out to everyone else who mattered to me up until that point, but my grandma was different. My gut told me she'd be fine, but what if she wasn't? What if my truth devastated her and she had a heart attack and died? What if her faith made her judge me and turn her back on me? I wasn't ready for any of these outcomes, but I no longer had a choice; I knew I had to speak to my grandma.

Looking back, I know exactly what I feared so much. My mom hadn't exactly responded well to my coming-out, and neither had my dad or my sister Kari, but I knew they'd come around. In my gut, I'd felt that with each of those relationships, we had the luxury of time to figure things out and repair any damage done by my revealing my truth.

My grandma was another story. On the off chance that she turned her back on me, I didn't know if we'd have time to rebuild a relationship, and as small as that chance might be, it wasn't one I was willing to take...until I was forced to take it.

I remember her loving me and telling me she didn't understand it but also assuring me that it would never affect the way she felt about me. I was her Poofenwaffer, and that would never change. Also, she felt compelled to tell me she watched the *Ellen Show* every day and that she really enjoyed her; representation matters.

My grandma was awesome.

Also, thank you, Ellen.

Busting out my best dance moves, trying to keep up
with my grandma. I told you she was awesome.

Not long after, I made the bold but terrifying decision to move
to New York City. I'd just graduated college after six and a half
short years and had convinced my boyfriend Jimmy to make the
move with me. We'd been given a couch and loveseat by a friend
to take with us, but they were both really ugly. I'm talking hideous
floral print and questionable cushion stains ugly! So I decided to
reupholster them. I'd never reupholstered anything in my life, but
I've always prided myself on being able to figure anything out,
so I was up for the challenge. I also knew it would be the perfect
opportunity to spend some time with my grandma before moving
away, so I asked her to help.

"Sure, honey. I don't know much about upholstering furniture,
but you can use my sewing machine, and I'm happy to help you make
some new throw pillows for it."

So, I spent my final week before moving to New York in my hometown, reupholstering furniture with my grandma. She got a kick out of watching me figure out how to cover these massive pieces of furniture. I set up shop in my parents' garage and spent entire days learning on the fly. Then it was time to make the matching throw pillows, which we'd decided to do at her apartment.

By this point, she was living alone not far from our house, so I tried spending as much time there with her as possible. I bought the materials I needed, and we got to work. She ended up on an oxygen tank less than a year or two later, so this is one of the last memories I have of my grandma healthy, vibrant, and fully mobile. I'll cherish it forever.

As we sat on the carpeted floor next to her kitchen table, where she'd often watched Ellen because old people have this weird love affair with eating dinner at like four o'clock, she asked me about my love life. Things were progressing quickly, and although I wasn't fully comfortable having this conversation with her, it felt good that she cared enough to ask.

"So, honey, tell me about Jimmy."

I get choked up even thinking about those words. For someone who has never known the struggle of coming out as gay, they might seem ordinary. For me, those words might as well have been, "I see you, I love you, you matter to me, and I want to know about this person in your life who brings you so much joy, because there isn't a thing on this planet that could make me stop caring about you."

I started talking about my boyfriend and didn't stop. I'd waited a long time to have this conversation with my Granny C, so I had a lot to tell her.

"Well, he's a gymnastics coach, he was a cheerleader at Ohio State, our friend Joe introduced us, I'm in love with him, we're moving to New York together…"

I went on and on.

She listened.

Then, she disappeared for a bit. When she returned, she was holding a large box.

"Honey, you said Jimmy just had a birthday last week. Well, I'd like you to give this to him."

My grandma handed me a black, wooden jewelry box. I recognized it from our family gift exchange the previous Christmas.

"I've already got one of these, and you said Jimmy likes to wear jewelry, so maybe he'll like this. I've got the box it came in somewhere, so we can make it look nice."

My grandma had just given my boyfriend a birthday gift! That was a MAJOR moment for me. Once again, she was leading by example and showing me that although she did not understand my relationship, she could see that it made me happy, and that was more important to her than anything else.

She was being a Christian.

I gave him the jewelry box, and as far as I know, he uses it to this day. Also, the couch and pillows turned out so nice! I learned the hard way that you need to put a slight curve in the corners of the pillows as you sew, or they'll look weird and pointy—just another thing my grandma Corky taught me that day.

Years later, as I wrapped up her eulogy and said my final goodbyes, stories like these and so many others warmed my heart and gave me the strength to give her the send-off she deserved.

You would not be reading this book if Grandma Corky had not taught me to love myself and to fight for my dreams. She really was the greatest, but now she's DEAD.

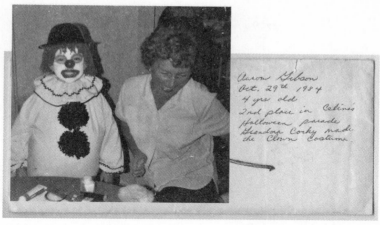

Aaron Gibson
Oct. 29th 1984
4 yrs old
2nd place in Celines
Halloween parade
Grandma Corky made
the Clown Costume

I joke about my grandma being dead, but the truth is that I know how very blessed I was to have had her in my life. Here, she made my entire Halloween costume from scratch. I was entered into the town costume contest and won second place. My prize: a $2 bill and a Snickers bar. I still have the $2 bill and the envelope it came in; I ate the Snickers. I miss my grandma every day.

Script Rewrites

Losing a loved one can be devastating. Few things in life have the ability to break our hearts like the loss of someone we care for deeply, but loss doesn't have to be a rock bottom moment.

The next time you are faced with a loss, try focusing on the joy that particular relationship brought into your life and showing gratitude for the memories. Also, I've found that a little humor can go a long way when grieving the loss of a loved one. People may think you're crazy if you start cracking jokes about every dead person you know, but find your version of funny and roll with it. You have my permission to be as sick and twisted as you want!

143

CHAPTER TEN:

CLOSETED AF

Scene 15: Four Gay Guys Walk Into a Bar...

INT. BAR — DAY

A beer mug slams down on a wooden table, spilling beer out onto the countertop.

The MAN holding the beer mug huddles over and LAUGHS as he slaps his knee. He brings the mug to his mouth once more and takes a long gulp.

The group of MEN sitting around the table are all a bunch of average-looking, middle-aged white guys.

The odd man out sitting with the group is AJ, aged twelve. He sits shyly at the side of the table glancing up occasionally at the TV behind the bar, totally ignoring the commotion in front of him.

A cigarette is put out into an ashtray, causing its smoke to rise into the air. It creates a fog around the group. The cigarette belongs to STEVE "GIBBY" GIBSON, AJ's father.

"Four gay guys walk into a bar and there is only one barstool, what do they do?"

"I don't know, Gibby, what do they do?" one of my dad's buddies replied.

"They flip it over!"

I'll never forget the day I heard my dad tell that joke. I'm talking about my real dad Steve here, not my stepdad Steve. Keep up! I think I was twelve or so and very much aware by that point in my life that I was a raging homo. I hadn't acted on it yet and was still years away from fully admitting that truth to myself or anyone else, but deep down, I knew exactly who I was. The awkward infatuations and uncomfortable sexual butterflies were popping up every time I was around the cool boys from school. Those confusing emotions weren't the only thing popping up, which was just brilliant! Why did God have to give young gay men a physical representation of the thing that we try so desperately to hide, especially in those younger years? I'm not saying I walk around now proudly showcasing my manhood, but we've become much closer now than we were back then. In those days, an awkward sign of arousal at the wrong moment could have resulted in me being harmed or even killed. This may sound dramatic, but it was very much my reality.

Beyond the constant fear of being "caught," I had to deal with my dad and his ignorant sense of humor. Gibby, as he's known, left no doubt how he felt about gays.

Hearing "jokes" like that from my dad at a time when literally everything was scary and confusing wasn't exactly fun. Also, that's just the *least* offensive gay joke I remember him telling and probably the only one I could put in print. If I shared with you half the things I heard come out of his mouth back then, he'd probably have LGBTQ rights groups on his front lawn with torches and pitchforks, and I'm not interested in all that. Actually, I think witty, well-thought-out messages on poster boards are more our style, but you get the idea.

Regardless, I was a terrified young kid who'd just heard his dad let the world know exactly how he felt about who I was inside.

My dad had no idea I was gay and wasn't trying to hurt me. I'm sure he thought he was just cracking a harmless joke. This was a long time before social media or political correctness became the norm. Back then, most people, especially white men from small towns, never really thought about how their words affected people; either that, or they just didn't care. I think it was probably a combination of the two.

His words affected me.

My parents had been divorced a few years by this point, and my dad had remarried for the fourth time. With that came a new stepmom and two new stepbrothers, neither of which I cared for too much. My insecurities were already through the roof every other weekend when my sister Kari and I had to go stay at our dad's house. He'd gotten a new family, and I felt left behind. I made it my job to protect my sister from all of that, but it hit me hard. If this was how my dad felt about gay people, I knew my ass was doomed. I wasn't sure there was any way to win him over, but that doesn't mean I didn't try.

My dad was always a great cook; it's how he expressed his love. It's one of my favorite things about him. I remember waking up to the best omelets and thinking my dad was a culinary genius. It didn't happen often, so when it did, I felt extra special and tried to study his every move so that I too could become a master in the kitchen. Most mornings, however, my sister and I had to choose some generic brand cereal. It's not that he couldn't afford the good stuff. Our stepmom locked the name-brand stuff in her bedroom closet when we came over for the weekend and only let our stepbrothers eat it, while we watched and choked down some random off-brand stuff from a black and white box. She was pretty awful in those early years, and it only added to the inner narrative I'd created in my mind. I was not worthy of my dad's love, and he would never accept me for who I was.

The truth wasn't too far from it.

My dad's one of those guys who blames everything on everyone else. He's never been big on accountability and likes to play the victim. I'm sure he would disagree, but he can tell you all his side of the story when *he* writes a book.

That was me being a smartass. I got that trait from BOTH sides of my family!

He's not a bad guy at all, and he loves his kids very much, but he is definitely a product of his environment. He didn't grow up in the most nurturing home, so he raised his children much as he was raised. Truth be told, we're very much alike in a lot of ways. I've never been a fan of accountability, and I spent most of my life wondering why the world handed me the short end of the stick, but I'm working on it, and so is he. Old habits die hard.

He was never a believer in things like emotions, the arts, or education. Basically, he was content to work in a factory, come home, throw back a few beers, and live a simple life. His weekends were usually filled with trips to the flea market and Indiana Hoosier basketball games, or if he really wanted to make our lives miserable, he'd put on some Nascar and we'd watch cars drive in circles for what seemed like an eternity.

I know the racetrack is actually an oval and people are really into it, but it was mind-numbing to me as a kid. Still, it's what my dad enjoyed, so I tried really hard to become a fan. To this day, I still tell people that I was named after Indy Car driver AJ Foyt—even though I have no idea if that's even true. My mom called me out for that recently, saying it's absurd and completely false, but I'm pretty sure I remember my dad saying it was true once when I was a little kid, and I think I held onto that. Until recently, I had no idea how much I actually loved my dad. I spent my teens and twenties convincing myself that I didn't need him, but that turned out to be easier said than done. All boys have a desire to be seen and respected by their fathers, and I'm no different. Maybe believing that he named me after a legend in the racing world made me feel closer to him, even though in reality, it has always felt like my dad and I were living on different planets.

For most of my life, I didn't really care what he thought of me or what his opinions of my life were. After my parents split, we only saw him every other weekend. That was the agreement that my parents came up with, and my sister Kari and I certainly preferred to live with our mom, but we still missed our dad. I wanted him to love me on a deeper level and understand the AJ that I was so afraid to reveal to him, but I never saw that as a possibility, so for my own sake, I kept my distance. I knew as I heard him tell those jokes that day when I was twelve that he was one of those people from whom I needed to protect myself. Mentally, I was rock solid. I would not open up to him and let him into the truest parts of myself. He would not break me.

Emotionally, my heart had different plans.

As much as I convinced myself that I did not care about my dad, so many parts of my life were influenced by his absence. The things I've held on to, though, are the times when he showed up for me, which usually revolved around sports. So I made a choice to play every sport and find ways to get him to notice me. I wasn't great at all of them, but he would still usually show up to support me. That was another way he expressed love. I remember this one time when he was there to watch me play wide receiver for our junior high football team. He had to stick around a bit longer than expected because I didn't really get much playing time until the fifth quarter.

Yeah, I know, the fifth quarter isn't actually a thing; neither was "The Good Witch of the South", a role my sister Kari played in the Immaculate Conception fifth grade production of *The Wizard of Oz*. But it's when I got a shot to play, so I took it. I really sucked at football. Like, I was really, really bad. I hated everything about it. I was fast, so I either played cornerback or wide receiver. There were legitimate problems with both.

Also, the thing about my sister was true too. She may have actually been worse at acting than I was at football, but the jury's still out on that.

Me in a football jersey, Kari as the Good Witch of the SOUTH! We weren't fooling anyone.

Back to my stellar football career.

On offense, I could run the routes and get open, but I couldn't catch the ball to save my damn life. Our first-string quarterback, Trent Dysert, threw the ball like he was trying to take out a brick wall, and I was not a fan of that. I preferred a softer, more subtle passing game. Not Trent. He was great, but those balls stung like hell!

On defense, I played cornerback. I could catch anyone, but that was the problem. The coaches knew I was fast, so it made sense to them that I should also play defense and run down receivers. I did that. And then I usually pretended to attempt to tackle them. I failed miserably. Running full speed and then throwing your body into someone else who is also running full speed and trying their best to NOT let you take them down is fun to watch on TV, but it sucks to do in person, especially if you're not a fan of pain, which I am not.

I recently watched some old footage with my family of a game where I was playing cornerback. I wasn't fooling anyone! My baby sis Kenzie loves to remind me of those videos from time to time. She wasn't even alive yet during my fifth-quarter glory days, but thanks to those VHS tapes, she's been able to get in on the inside family joke of making fun of my time on the gridiron. Not cool, sis...not cool at all!

Needless to say, the whole cornerback thing didn't really take. So, running routes as a wide receiver in the fifth quarter was my time to shine. By that point, the backup quarterback, Justin Rolfes, was in the game, and his balls didn't carry quite the same sting as Trent's, so his were catchable for me. I was still terrified every single time the ball was thrown anywhere remotely near me. I hated every minute on that football field, but both of my parents seemed to enjoy it, so I stuck with it. To this day I'm still not sure if my dad actually came to see me play or if he was there for my stepbrother, who was also in my grade and on the same team. He was pretty terrible, too, so I can't imagine my dad had too much fun either way.

The summer before high school, I remember thinking that maybe I'd continue to play into my freshman year and see how things went. My family thought I was talented and really wanted to see how I developed athletically as a player. My mom forced me to get my summer physical and told me I had to play a sport in the fall. If I decided against football, she told me I had to try out for soccer. I hadn't played soccer in years, so that was never going to happen. And as much as I hadn't enjoyed football in junior high, I did like the idea of seeing if I could become good at it in high school. I actually believed that I could be pretty awesome, but there was a major problem, one I've never told anyone in my life until now.

I promised to be honest, so here goes.

I was told that in high school, football players showered together after practice. As hot as that might've seemed to a young gay boy in theory, the idea terrified me in reality. I can actually feel my heart racing now as I type this, recalling how afraid I was of being "outed" at that age. I imagined myself getting aroused in the shower and ending up dead. I could actually see my bloody body lying lifeless on the locker room floor, and the image petrified me. I'm sure that seems dramatic to some, but small towns are no joke when it comes to things like sexuality, and in 1995, that fear was very real. So real that it kept me from exploring my potential as a football player. I decided that playing football just wasn't in the cards for me. I'd have to find another way to get my dad to pay attention to me, preferably one that didn't involve me getting pummeled on a field or in the locker room.

My mom was furious when I told her I wasn't going to play any sports in the fall of my freshman year, but that's how it had to be. Explaining my reasoning would've been far worse than dealing with her anger over what she perceived as my laziness. I was okay with looking lazy, and my secret remained safely hidden from the world.

I wish my mom had been the type of parent we see in movies and on TV shows nowadays; you know, the one who loves and supports her son regardless of something like his sexuality. That just wasn't the case. I know she regrets that now and would not even recognize the woman she was back then. She was a jock in high school, so she raised her children the only way she knew how: to love sports.

I was still a huge fan of watching football, and just like my dad, the Miami Dolphins were my team. Later that fall, possibly as a way to show my mom that I was still into football and throw her further off my track, I relentlessly sent entries to a contest being held by General Mills or Post or one of the other major cereal brands. They were rewarding a certain number of submissions with two tickets to an NFL game, and I was determined to win. To clarify, these were cereals bought by my actual mom, because of, you know, the whole stepmom locking the good stuff in the closet thing. Anyway, I submitted entries over and over, and finally one day, I got a letter in the mail with two tickets! They were for an upcoming game against the Colts at the old RCA Dome in Indianapolis. I was beside myself. The only problem: I'd been too afraid to tell my mom of my master plan because I thought she'd flip, and too afraid to tell my dad either, because I didn't think I would win, and then I'd just be a failure once again.

Well, I had won, and now I had to convince my mom to let my dad, who she'd never really been much a fan of, take me to Indianapolis, which was three hours away, in the winter. The Midwest in the wintertime can be a scary place. Snowstorms pop up out of nowhere, and even on clear days, there's always that infamous "black ice" that everyone says you can't see, but which causes wipeouts left and right. I'm sure there's truth to that, but I didn't care. I was going to bro out with my dad; my stepfamily was not invited, and THIS was going to be the day our relationship changed forever…if my mom didn't shut it down.

She said yes. I called my dad, and he was totally pumped. This was going more smoothly than I could have ever imagined. He said we were going to grab lunch at this place called Hooters beforehand and then head to the game. I had no idea what that meant. I just knew that my dad and I were going to see the Miami Dolphins!

I told mom and she lost her shit, so we never got to go to Hooters. In hindsight, maybe she should've let him take me so the sight of all those gorgeous women in skimpy outfits could've piqued my interest and saved me from this life of sin, because you know that's how that works.

Fun side note, my mom ended up taking me to a Hooters later that year when we went to St. Louis to watch my cousin Jenny's cheerleading competition. I think she just enjoyed saying no to my dad. The food was bad, and let's just say I was more concerned with the tackiness of those hideous uniforms than I was with what was underneath them.

Back to the football game.

We had a blast and even got to see Dan Marino break the all-time touchdown record that day. It was one of the coolest experiences of my young life and one of the few things I'd ever done with my dad alone. To this day, I can only think of one other time my dad and I have ever been alone together, which kind of sucks, but I'd broken the pattern and started to build a relationship with him. We'd finally connected over sports.

I'd already been playing sports since I was about five, so going all in wasn't that much of a leap for me. I loved competing. I'm sure I was competing as much for my dad's attention as I was for the actual sport I was playing, but the distinction wasn't obvious to me back then. I worked as hard as I could to prove my talent, my worthiness, and probably my manhood to my dad, and I was rewarded for it every time he showed up to one of my sporting events. From the time I was five until I graduated high school, I participated in soccer, baseball, football, swimming, volleyball, tennis, basketball, cross-country, and track and field. Each was at different stages of my youth, but I was always playing at least one or two sports per season, year-round. And for the most part, my dad showed up to support me.

Real talk, it was also a great way to hide the fact that I was actually a big homo, because back then the idea of a gay man also being athletic wasn't even something small-town folk could wrap their brains around, my dad included. In my mind, he could never know.

As I got older, I realized that he tended to show up more often and stay longer at the sporting events where I was actually really good. In high school, I ran track, and I was pretty badass. I ran hurdles, and I was the best on our team from my sophomore year until I graduated. My specialty, the 110-meter-high hurdles, was always one of the first events of the meet, and my dad would show up early, come over and wish me luck, and then stand along the edge of the fence in front of the bleachers to cheer me on. My mom and stepdad were always in the stands, but my dad was right there by my side. I loved that.

Eventually, though, I started noticing a pattern. I also ran the 300-meter hurdles and anchored the 4 x 100-meter relay (not because I was the fastest, but mostly because the other three guys could get me a lead, and I was so afraid of losing it that I ran like a cheetah, or probably more like a gazelle). I wasn't lightning fast, but I was fast, and the anchor of the relay gets the baton pretty late and really only runs about ninety meters, so I'm pretty sure that factored in. You know where I didn't run though…in the B relay! The B relay is track and field's version of the imaginary fifth quarter of a football game, so I was making progress athletically.

What I noticed was that my dad, my biggest supporter in the event that I almost always won, would "peace out" before my other events. Not always, but more often than not he would come up with an excuse why he needed to leave or just simply slip away after my marquee event. That hurt. I was never man enough to express that emotion to him back then, but it showed me a couple of things. First, he was only willing to support me when I was the best at something, when I was the athlete or the person he wanted me to be. Secondly, he liked to be right up front when I ran so all of the town could see what a great dad he was. It was more about him than it was about me.

Both realities hit deep, and I dealt with neither until much later in life, which is what many of us do when it comes to complex relationship challenges, especially ones involving close family members. My dad wasn't a bad person, but he was definitely a selfish person and not a great father. I learned at a very young age the difference between a dad and being a father, and he was certainly not the latter.

To be fair, much of that came from the way he was raised. In a family of all boys, he's actually the most loving and the most willing to have a conversation of substance. My uncles on his side aren't really the type of men to show love or compassion. They were raised by two different fathers, both with drinking problems, a vice that was definitely passed on to my dad. He's been a textbook alcoholic his entire adult life, but not in the way you see portrayed on film or in TV shows. I've never seen my dad drink a drop of liquor, and he never laid a hand on me and rarely even raised his voice. He just likes to drink beer. A lot of beer.

Not just any beer, he drinks Busch Light. It's basically chilled piss water, which tells me it's more about the addiction than the taste. My dad continued the only cycle he'd ever known, so it's hard to blame him for raising his children the way that he was raised. He also married four different women and had multiple kids, so there are definitely more layers to his story. I can't imagine what that must've been like for him, but I know what it felt like to be a closeted teenage boy trying desperately to be the best athlete I could be to win my dad's attention and then seeing him leave every time my best event was over. It knocked the wind out of me without fail.

By the age of twenty, as a sophomore at the University of Toledo, I began to come out to some close friends and eventually some family members. I wasn't ready to reveal myself to my dad because I knew exactly how he'd respond, and that wasn't a burden I was ready or able to bear. Things rarely go as planned.

I was relaxing in my dorm room one night, probably making ramen noodles or chatting with a boy on ICQ (that's how old I am), when I got a phone call from my dad. I'd never given him my number and still have no idea how he got it, but I knew shit was about to get real. Either someone important had died or he knew my secret.

No one had died.

"Well, I've been hearing some things about you, and I just need you to tell me they're not true. I've been hearing you're gay. That's not true, is it?"

Friendly public service announcement: if you ever hear your child might be a member of the LGBTQ community, this is not the way to approach the situation. My advice would be to focus on creating a safe, healthy environment for children to discover themselves and reveal their personal truth to you on their own time and in their own way. Ambushes are rarely a good idea, especially when they're done this way.

"Well, dad, actually, I am gay."

My world was spinning out of control, and I couldn't believe I'd actually answered honestly.

"Are you sure?"

"Yeah, dad, I'm pretty sure."

"Oh, okay. I just wanted to hear it from you."

"Okay, Dad..."

Click. The conversation was over.

My dad wouldn't say the word "gay" to me again for another fifteen years. I can't even put into words how that felt; I've got some baggage.

Years later, after attending three different colleges over the course of six and a half years, I was ready to receive my diploma. The coming-out process was traumatic for me and led to a lot of quitting on myself and some bad decision-making, which explains my extended college experience. I struggled with a lot of demons during this time, and the fact that I even survived this period of my life amazes me to this day. I did a lot of self-discovery during those years. I lost my virginity on a bedroom floor in Rossford, Ohio, had my first boyfriend (that came after the losing my virginity part), had my heart broken for the first time, and wore eyeliner to more than a few gay clubs (I looked great with a smoky eye). I was definitely figuring some stuff out. I was so broken in my early twenties, but I fought for my life, and I survived.

At the age of twenty-five, I was about to receive my bachelor's degree in communications from THE Ohio State University. It is still one of the greatest accomplishments of my life, and I wanted my entire family there to witness my special moment.

My dad had never supported college, because he thought it was a waste of time and money. I'm not sure what route he thought I should take, but higher education was definitely not something he valued and certainly not something he would help pay for. He never contributed a dime to my education. Still, I was proud that I had actually tricked one of the largest universities in the country into giving me a degree. I had obviously done something right!

I wanted my family there, but scheduling events like this in a split family has always been complicated. Damn you, Divorce! Not really, though, because it was one of the best things that ever happened to my sister Kari and me, but it made big days like this one so awkward.

I'm sort of a maniac when it comes to planning and itineraries, so this was a chance to put my neuroses to work. I worked as a server at a couple of restaurants in college that were both located close to campus, so I decided I would go to breakfast with my dad's side of the family before graduation and go to dinner with my mom's side after. My dad has always been more of a morning person anyway, so this would be perfect. Problem solved!

My dad had never come to visit me at any of my colleges, so this was a big deal. I decided we'd go to brunch at Champps Americana, sit on the patio and have a beautiful family meal to kick off the big day. We did and other than a side comment about the cost of the bill, my dad was wonderful and on his best behavior. I wanted to tell him that my stepdad had dished out close to $20,000 for my college education, so the cost of my eggs Benedict should really be no concern of his, but I bit my tongue. I regret that decision.

I was graduating in the springtime, so our ceremony was held indoors at St. John Arena. It's old but iconic, and two-time Heisman winner Archie Griffin was speaking to the graduates, so I thought my dad would love that. My dad's a Michigan fan, but talent is talent! He sat with my stepmom, my older sister Chris, and my brother-in-law Jerry on one side of the arena while my parents sat with my sister Kari and my boyfriend Jimmy on the other. Jimmy's mother had died earlier that week after a long battle with lupus and had been buried that morning, but he knew how important this day was to me, so he drove three hours back to Columbus to be there to support me. I'll always be grateful for that.

As the emcee announced the school of communications and asked us to rise so they could announce our names one by one, I looked up into the stands with the deepest pride I'd ever felt. I had overcome every obstacle, I'd come out to my family, I'd dropped out of school twice, and I'd gotten over my eyeliner phase, and I had still been able to pick myself back up and earn my diploma. This was a major victory for me. I could see my mom, stepdad, sister, and boyfriend all cheering for me, snapping pictures that would never turn out all the way from the nosebleed seats. More names were called, and then I was only a few spots from walking up onto that stage, hearing my name, and receiving my diploma. My heart was racing. I was so proud of myself and so grateful that my dad had finally stuck around to support me, even though he was not front and center and would receive no recognition on this day. I glanced up one last time, because every kid wants to know their parents are watching their biggest successes.

As I located my dad and stepmom high in the auditorium, while I was just moments from receiving my diploma, I realized they looked different this time. They were still standing, but their backs were to me. Three graduates in front of me, two graduates, my dad was gone. He had walked out of the ceremony. My heart began to beat out of control, tears burst from my eyes, and my body went numb. My hearing felt muffled, and as I realized there was no longer a line in front of me, I knew it was my turn to step onto that stage and receive my diploma. I was in full-on panic mode, but I was doing my best to hide it, well, because toxic masculinity.

This was the single proudest moment of my life, and my dad had once again stripped the joy from the moment. My big sister and her husband remained, but my dad never saw me receive my diploma.

Typical.

I had opened my heart and invited him in, and then he'd made my graduation about him. I would not make that mistake again.

My sister Kari and me the day I graduated
from THE Ohio State University. My dad
was long gone by this point, but I was
filled with pride. GO BUCKS!

I pretended like it didn't matter and that he hadn't hurt me. I probably believed that lie at the time. For years, I was okay with the distance between us. He never accepted my sexuality, but I kept doing my best to shove it in his face. On multiple occasions, after I'd graduated and moved on to New York and eventually Los Angeles, I would call to tell my dad I'd be coming home for a visit and asked if he'd like to have dinner. Like I said earlier, he's great in the kitchen and almost always prefers to make a meal and spend time together in his home. I often brought whoever I was dating at the time home with me, and on multiple occasions, I remember my dad asking if I could come out to his house alone.

My answer was always no. I knew he was uncomfortable with my sexuality, but I was not about to let him avoid it forever.

"Dad, I'm not going to leave my boyfriend, who flew cross-country to spend time with my family, sitting alone while I come to your house for dinner. That's rude."

"Okay, bring him."

My dad was uncomfortable, but he wasn't a bad person. At least his desire to see me was greater than his disdain for that part of my life. These were small victories.

For years, this continued. He never addressed my sexuality or asked about my relationships, and I never let him know how that made me feel. We remained in a weird sort of purgatory for fifteen years. Then, he got a taste of discrimination himself, and with it came a shift in perspective.

He'd retired and decided to spend much of his free time reconnecting with some old work buddies. They would go golfing five days a week, throw back a few beers, and shoot the shit. They would carpool, probably for safety reasons, and on one car ride home, one of his buddies started talking about this "faggot" from our home town.

"Did you see that article in the paper about that faggot from Celina that got a talk show on Fox?"

My dad said, "Excuse me?"

"Yeah, that Steve Kuhn at Reynolds & Reynolds got a faggot for a son, and he's getting a TV show. If I had a faggot for a son, I'd kill him!"

Well, there weren't too many gay guys from my hometown with TV shows, so it was clear that this beautiful human being was referring to me. Also, remember the whole two dads named Steve thing? I may have forgotten to mention that they both worked at the same factory in my hometown. My stepdad was actually my dad's boss. That was awkward, but not nearly as awkward as this conversation was for my dad.

"Yeah, that faggot's dad did work at Reynolds, but it's Steve Gibson, and who the hell are you to talk about my son that way?"

They never played golf together again.

My dad told me this story a few weeks later when I was home for a visit, and two things happened that I'd never before experienced. He said the word "gay" to me for the first time in fifteen years, and he cried in front of me for the first time in my life. In that moment, every wall I'd ever built came crashing down. Much like the walls I'd built to protect myself from religion crumbled the first time I set foot in a church after fifteen years, these walls did the exact same thing, also after fifteen years.

He said that the moment he heard his buddy talking about his son that way, he felt a rage and had to defend me. My dad also said that for the first time since I'd come out to him, he thought to himself, "Hmmm, I wonder how this has affected AJ?"

I was blown away. My dad had said the words that I'd waited a lifetime to hear. I'd built walls so high and so thick that I had convinced myself he could never penetrate them. Much like the fifteen-year period during which I'd told myself I was an atheist, when I was really just protecting myself from getting hurt by people using God's name to judge and condemn me, I'd spent the fifteen years since coming out to my dad denying how badly I wanted him to accept me too.

I'm actually realizing the correlation as I type these words, and I'm feeling an overwhelming sense of God's love filling my soul. For fifteen years, I hid from God because of all the heartache I'd endured at the hands of Christians. For fifteen years, I shut off feelings for my dad in order to get through life not feeling like a failure as a son. The irony is that in both scenarios, I was avoiding a relationship with my father; one heavenly, one earthly, but both essential to my personal well-being and wholeness as a man. Once again, God has used brokenness in my familial relationships to teach me the truest meaning of the word love.

I love my dad. Our journey has not always been a smooth one, but I understand him so much more as an adult than I ever could as a child. He was not perfect, no parent is, but over time he has grown into someone that I love and appreciate deeply. I'm so grateful for that. I'm also grateful for that narrow-minded man that day in the car. If it had not been for him, my dad might never have accepted his "faggot" son, and we might never have healed our relationship, and I might never have sat down to write this story, and God might never have revealed himself to me in this way.

A complete life is made up of a series of highs and lows; relationships that teach us, relationships that hurt us, and sometimes, relationships that make us better. The close ones, the ones that matter, have the power to heal us if we are open to the process. For me, my relationship with my dad is one that has brought me much unexpected joy the past couple of years, and I pray that we have many more years to build on the progress we've made. Also, my stepmom is pretty cool now, too, and has apologized for hiding the good cereal in the early days of her marriage to my dad. She, too, was struggling to find her place in a new family dynamic, and now I love her dearly. She also played an important role in helping my dad comprehend and come to terms with my sexuality. For that, I will always be grateful.

As for my dad, he doesn't tell gay jokes anymore.

I consider that progress.

Script Rewrites

It's unfortunate that my dad and I were such bad communicators for so many years, but if it's something we could figure out, then it's something ANY two people can figure out. Recently, during a workshop in Denver, I participated in something called "Walk2Connect." It's a grassroots organization aimed at getting people moving again and encouraging them to connect with others from their community in the process. It was an awesome experience!

Their motto is "Life at 3 mph," and their aim is to slow things down and create spaces to clear the mind so that we can reconnect with the people and places that surround us every day. We were challenged to pair up and get to know someone new. I walked with this incredible human being named Sarai and we had the most wonderful conversation. She'd been raised evangelical Christian but had later found a different, healthier relationship with God and had allowed that process to transform not only her heart, but her life. I know this, because I was given the opportunity to ask. We were given a simple but rare gift during our walk together, and that was the freedom to get to know each other with no parameters or expectations. I loved every minute of it, and her kindness made me a better man that day.

This simple exercise had such a profound impact on me that I've decided to bring it to you. So here's my challenge. Hit up someone in your life who you'd like to know more about, ask them to join you for a walk, and then on the walk, take turns asking each other questions. I'd like you to agree to ask and answer no less than twenty questions each during your walk and see what you learn about each other. The first few questions might be a little superficial, and that's okay, but as you continue to walk and discover awesome little nuggets about each other, the conversation will expand, and so will your understanding of each other.

I spent so many years not understanding my own father because I was too afraid to communicate with him and because he was too afraid to share. I challenge you to not make the same mistakes my father and I made. Nature is one of God's ways of speaking to us, so don't be afraid to take stock of your surroundings during your walk and share what you're experiencing. You may discover you're not the only one eager to connect on a deeper level.

CHAPTER ELEVEN:

OUTED AF

Scene 24: Bi Bi Closet.

INT. AJ'S CHILDHOOD HOME — LIVING ROOM — DAY

On the screen of an old TV is a fuzzy
recording of a song and dance show. The
performance takes place in front of the
iconic Cinderella castle. The purple lights
of the giant castle engulf the dancers as
they perform.

Watching the home recording from the couch
is STEVE, AJ's stepfather, who is holding
KENZIE, AJ's four-year-old sister.

Sitting on the floor are KATHY, AJ's mother,
and a twenty-year-old AJ, his confidence
suppressed by his nervous demeanor.

My parents had recently taken my little sister Kenz to Disneyworld for the first time and wanted to show me the family videos they'd taken during the trip. I drove home from college to spend a few hours with them, do some laundry, and grab a free meal. Mom took the opportunity to show me everything they'd done, including the live shows they'd seen.

"This was a really neat performance in front of Cinderella's castle! It was only fifteen minutes or so, but they sang and they danced their little hearts out. So many talented kids, I could see you doing something like this, but I'm pretty sure some of them were gay."

Why did my mom feel the need to mention that last part, as if it were relevant to the story? What on earth did the sexuality of those dancers have to do with anything? I was confused, but mostly annoyed. More often than not, when I'm annoyed with my mom, I blurt out some sort of retort, hoping to make her aware of whatever absurd thing she'd just said.

"Mom, I think I'm bi."

WHOA! Not the response I was looking for! Had I just come out to my mom? I'd thought about this moment a million times, but did NOT see it going like this!

My mom went on the offensive. "What do you mean you're bi? What does that even mean?"

"I don't know, Mom. I mean, I just know that I'm attracted to guys too, but maybe I still like girls. I'm not really sure what it means yet."

I knew my mom wouldn't take this news well, which is why I'd waited twenty years to share it. Coming out was the scariest thing I'd ever done, and as my mom processed what I'd just told her, I could see it was not going well.

"Honey, how do you know you're bi or whatever? You're only twenty, you have no idea what you like yet."

That statement could not have been further from the truth. I knew exactly what I liked, and I liked boys. Actually, I liked boys A LOT! I'd liked boys since the time I fooled around with a classmate of mine in our basement at the age of six or seven. I'd never shared that with her or anyone else out of respect for the boy, but we knew exactly what we were doing and both enjoyed it. Of course, it was more of an exploratory thing back then and less about sexual pleasures, because, well, we were children, but I do remember how comfortable we both were.

"Mom, I just know. I don't know how to explain it, but I just do."

I was lying through my teeth. I'd known for over a decade that I was a full-on homo! There was nothing bi about me. I believe that all humans fall somewhere on the spectrum and knew that I was 100 percent raging homosexual, but using the word bi felt like the safest way to start this conversation with my mom. In hindsight, it probably gave her some level of false hope, but I was more interested in not being shunned by my family than I was concerned for my mom's feelings at the time.

Also (and this is a good note for all parents whose children trust them enough to reveal the most vulnerable parts of themselves, whether it be regarding their sexuality or anything else not considered "normal" by traditional societal standards), IT'S NOT ABOUT YOU!

Apparently, my mom hadn't gotten that memo.

"Do you know how stupid this makes me look, honey? People have been hearing things and asking me about you, and I've defended you every single time. I feel so stupid right now!"

Awesome. My mom was clearly grasping how difficult this was for me. She stormed off to the back sunroom and lit up a cigarette. It was the only room in the house where she was allowed to smoke (she's since quit, thank God). As she stared out the back window, puffing away on her American Spirits, my stepdad Steve, who'd been sitting there quietly the entire time, decided to get in on this difficult family moment.

"So, are you seeing anyone?"

I couldn't believe it. My Pops was asking me if I had a boyfriend!

"Yeah, actually. His name is Brian, and we met on New Year's Eve. I think I'm in love."

THIS was the conversation I desperately wanted to have with my mom. She clearly wasn't ready, but Steve was. It's hard to put words to the emotions that I felt in that moment. I'd been hiding this part of myself for nearly fifteen years, and as I revealed my truth, I was met with two extremely different reactions.

My mom had reacted out of a place of fear. Her ego was bruised, and she was afraid of what others might think of her.

My stepdad showed me nothing but love in that moment. I needed that. Had he reacted in the same manner as my mom, I'm not sure how my story would have turned out. To be honest, I'm not sure I'd be here today to talk about it. In some ways, I believe that his reaction that day saved my life, and I'm not sure I've ever really told him that. I guess I'm telling him now, assuming that he reads this book.

Also, there's a zero percent chance my Pops won't read this book! He still has the program from my fifth grade performance of *Peter Pan*, autographed by me. I played the role of John Darling, but to him, I was the star, and he wanted to be able to say one day that he had my very first autograph. He's been a superfan for years; he's TOTALLY reading this book!

So, thanks, Pops, for choosing love that day and for helping Mom through that time. I know it wasn't easy for her.

As for my relationship with my mom, it took a while to heal. She didn't speak to me for the next month, which has never happened before or since. It was rough. I know she talked to Steve about the truth I'd revealed, but she wasn't quite ready to talk to me. When she finally was ready, it wasn't pretty.

"Honey, you know I love you. I'm just embarrassed and I'm worried about you. I'm worried what others will say about you, I'm worried this will make your life harder, I'm worried that you'll never get to be a dad, I'm worried you'll get AIDS and die…"

Holy shit, my mom was worried about a lot! I'd been out to my friends for a few months by the time I told my parents, and not one of them had ever brought up these concerns with me. Every one of my friends had been nothing but supportive. I'd spent the recent holiday break with my old crew, and they had been so awesome.

When I told my friend Hiedi, lying under the stars out by the lake as the clock struck midnight on my twentieth birthday, her response was, "Yeah, so? I always kind of figured."

My buddy Ben and I were driving through a bank ATM one night to take out cash to buy some cigarettes (I smoked every now and then back then, sue me!), and he asked why I'd been acting weird lately, which prompted me to blurt out, "Ben, I'm gay!"

He said, "Cool, I don't care."

We got our cash, bought cigarettes, and headed to a party at our friend Jenna's house.

My friend Elena was going to Ohio State, and I was staying with her for the weekend. We were getting ready to go out for the night. I had a crush on her friend John and knew I'd have a hard time hiding that from her after we got to drinking later that evening, so I felt compelled to tell her while we were both still sober.

I told her, she didn't care at all, and our friendship only grew stronger from there. I ended up going home with John later that night, so it's probably a good thing we had that talk BEFORE all that went down.

Mom and Elena cheering me on during a volleyball
tournament at OSU, the morning after I hooked up
with Elena's best friend John. Mom didn't know and
Elena didn't care. Apparently, she didn't care about
her style, either. LOL.

The next night, while we were getting ready to go out again, she
called me into her room. "AJ, if you were a guy, would you think I
looked hot in this?"

"Bitch, I am a guy!"

We both started laughing.

"You know what I meant!"

I did know what she meant and took zero offense at her slipup.
We'd been friends for years, and this was no different than the
million ridiculous conversations we'd had before. I didn't take

offense because I knew she still loved me and I was grateful that our relationship hadn't changed.

I wish I could say the same for my relationship with my mom.

The months following that day in our living room were some of the scariest in my life. None of my friends shared the same concerns as my mom, but that didn't stop those fears from slowly creeping into my own image of myself and my future.

One night, while staying with my boyfriend Brian in Columbus for the weekend, I decided to write my mom an email. We were barely communicating at the time, and I needed to fix that. My friends and I had just seen the movie *Requiem for a Dream*, and it had left us all emotional wrecks. I decided it was a good time to get everything I needed to say to my mom out, so I sat down at my friend Joe's aqua blue iMac and poured my heart out. I remember apologizing over and over again for upsetting her, for being a disappointment, and for making her look bad. It was more important to me to have my mom in my life than it was for me to live as my authentic self, so I took on all of her emotional handicaps as problems of my own.

It wasn't the healthiest choice, but it did get us communicating again and helped my mom to see for the first time how deeply tortured I was by my sexuality and more importantly, by her hurtful reaction to my truth.

While we were struggling to navigate this new relationship as mother and son, my sister Kari was busy being a high schooler. She was playing club volleyball that winter, and our parents had hired a personal scout to help her get noticed by colleges.

This scout, I believe his name was Scott, would email my mom updates all of the time, letting her know who he'd been in contact with and which colleges were interested in Kari. From time to time, Kari would sign into mom's account to check emails from Scott.

I hadn't considered that the night I sat sobbing at my friend's computer.

Just as things began to settle with my mom, I got a call from her for which I was not prepared.

"Honey, your sister knows you're gay."

She was still a teenager living in a small town and the center of my universe; I was NOT ready for her to know. I felt violated. I felt betrayed.

"Mom, why on earth would you tell Kari? I never said I was ready to talk to her about this yet!"

I was not taking the news well.

"Honey, I didn't tell her. She was in my email account checking for updates from her scout and she saw the email you'd sent me. She read it; I'm sorry."

Okay, so not only did my sister know that I was gay, she had found out by reading an email that I wrote at the most desperate, lowest point in my life. I had apologized profusely for even *being* gay, and THAT is what my sister had read. So, did Kari now think I was doing something wrong by living as my authentic self? Would she react the same way as mom had?

"Well, what did she say, Mom?"

"Honey, she's still in high school, and you know how people are around here. She doesn't understand it, and I'm sure she doesn't agree with it, but she's still your sister."

"Okay, Mom. But did you try telling her I'm still me and that's never going to change? Does she know I still love her and I'm still her big brother?"

"Yes, honey. I told her all of that. I told her that all those things that she loves so much about you, the things that you two share that none of her girlfriends share with their older brothers, that maybe you share those things because you're different and because you're more in touch with your emotions than most straight guys."

My mom was right. Kari and I had a unique bond. I just hoped desperately that she would hold onto that as she navigated the reality that she had a gay big brother.

It would take a while, but eventually Kari did come around, and what had been embarrassing for her as a teenager became something she was very proud of by the time she graduated high school. She spent time visiting me in college, getting to know the guys I was dating and going out to gay clubs with me. Sure, I was sneaking her in with fake IDs, but we were having a blast, and more importantly, we were building a new relationship.

The walls had been torn down, and we were getting to know each other all over again as adults. The next decade of our relationship would take us to New York, Los Angeles, and eventually to that sidewalk outside Lemonade. We still fought like brothers and sisters do, but at the end of the day we always supported each other because we understood the importance of family. She is my only full-blooded sibling, and that has always bonded us in a unique way, but it's also why we've always been able to hurt each other so deeply over the years.

Family dynamics are complicated, and I know our story is far from over, but I do wish I'd had the opportunity to come out to my sister on my own terms all those years ago. Maybe if I'd been able to express to her how I was truly feeling inside instead of her reading an apology letter to my mom sent out of desperation, things might be different now. Unfortunately, I'll never know.

As for my mom, she is my biggest fan and a staunch supporter of the LGBTQ community. She loves me and understands that my sexuality is a gift from God. Our souls are connected in a way I cannot fully describe, but it is a way that would not have been possible if I hadn't revealed my truth, if she hadn't taken the time to process her emotions about my truth, and if we hadn't built a new relationship around that truth. She is my best friend, and I am so grateful that God decided to make her my mom. Also, I'm pretty sure she's grateful for getting such a dope son!

Script Rewrites

If you haven't picked up on this by now, I'm a huge fan of authentically connecting with people and places. So with that in mind, I'd like you to reach out to someone who has been a positive role model in your life. This person might be your mom, but it might also be an aunt or uncle, a grandparent, a special teacher, or a coach. Whoever this person is, reach out and invite them out to lunch, dinner, or for a cup of coffee.

Sit with them, ask them about their childhood, find out who was a positive role model in their life, and take in their stories. We are all deeply connected, but it's important that we create spaces every now and then that allow for those connections to be revealed. So create the space; through finding out how your role model became so special, you will better understand yourself and how you can do better for the people looking to you as a role model. Have fun with this.

CHAPTER TWELVE:

FRUSTRATED AF

Scene 82: Momma Kath, Sister Sledge and the Triangle of Doom

INT. HOUSE — LIVING ROOM — EARLY MORNING

The clock TICKS on, matching rhythm with the impatient tapping of AJ's finger against his crossed arms.

Placed at AJ's feet are multiple packed suitcases and a sleeping pillow.

His brow furrows as he checks the time on his iPhone.

MACKENZIE, AJ's little sister, and STEVE, AJ's stepfather, are slouched on the couches, looking put-out.

    STEVE

  Kath!

    MACKENZIE

  Mom, we have to go!

KATHY, AJ's mom, comes scurrying around the corner into the living room.

    KATHY

  Give me a few more minutes!

Momma Kath's trademark phrase has always been, "Give me a few more minutes." If she becomes famous on social media someday, we're totally printing shirts with those six words plastered across the front.

My mom has a long, well-documented history of never being on time to anything and always waiting until the very last minute to get ready. It's a skill set I, too, picked up somewhere along the way and have recently fought hard to correct.

She has not.

My mom was so excited about this trip. We were all heading to Nashville to see our cousin Daisy get married. Much of our extended family, who we rarely see anymore, would be there, and I'm sure that as my mom finished packing, they were in her thoughts. I know my mom, and I'm sure she wanted to look and feel her best in front of her cousins and their families. I get that. Also, none of us had ever been to Nashville, so she really wanted to get the full experience. I've learned as an adult that the "full" experience means something very different to my parents than it means to me.

I'm the type of guy who likes to do some light research (a full-on case study) and have a general plan (ten page itinerary) whenever I know there are things I want to accomplish on a trip. My parents, not so much. Let me paint a picture for you.

Earlier in the week I'd asked what time we'd be leaving for Nashville, and Momma Kath made it very clear that she'd like to leave early because she wanted to spend the entire day getting to see the city. My stepdad took the day off work, and my sister got the okay to miss her only college course later that afternoon, so we had a game plan and we were ready to put it into action. In my mind, we were about to go full-on honky-tonk for the next forty-eight hours.

I knew I'd be eating lots of barbecue and drinking more than my fair share of bourbon over the weekend, so I wanted to be prepared. I asked if I'd be able to take this workout class before we left that would end at 6:45 a.m. Nothing in our hometown is more than a five-minute drive in any direction, so I didn't see a problem with this plan.

Kathy saw it differently.

"I want to be on the road at 7 a.m.!"

Okay, cool. I asked if she thought it would be possible to get on the road at 7:15 so I could shower after this class. Initially, she'd said no. Since she didn't have an actual reason or any sort of schedule that we needed to stick to, I told her that her response was a bit irrational. That didn't go over too well.

My mom had set a completely arbitrary departure time in her head, and nothing was going to convince her to adjust it. If you've ever had to take your parents to the airport and had your dad insist that they needed to be there seventeen hours before their flight "in case security is backed up," then you can relate. This was one of THOSE situations.

She got really upset, because time crunches that could've been avoided but weren't always stress Kathy, so I said it was fine, I wouldn't work out. So, in classic Momma Kath fashion, she then decided it would be okay for me to take the class.

P.S. It drives my mom crazy when I call her Kathy, but I'm pretty sure she also kind of likes it. Some people might think that's disrespectful. I'm not one of them.

Her house, her rules. I get it.

I've played this game with my mom a million times in my life, and I know that it has nothing to do with our actual departure time and everything to do with her being in charge. She likes to feel like she makes the decisions, and in her mind, she's totally justified. I'm a grown-ass man, but I don't know if she'll ever actually see me that way. She told me that we could leave at 7:15, but if I were a minute late, they'd be leaving my ass behind. (Her words, except of course she said "your" instead of "my," but this is my first book, and I'm not really sure of the grammar on that, but you get the picture.) Again, this was her way of asserting her control over this new, adjusted departure time.

I knew that would never happen. I also knew she'd never be ready to go at 7:15. Regardless, just to be safe, I canceled the class to ease her stress levels because they tend to be pretty epic. I got up around 6:15 am, cleaned the bedroom I'd been staying in and the two bathrooms I'd been using, packed my luggage into the back of the car, and took my bedding down to the laundry room, then at 7:15 am, I sat next to my little sister on the couch...and we waited.

Well 7:30 rolled around, and still there was no sign of Kathy. At 7:45, and my stepdad was ready; I mentioned as lightheartedly and with the least amount of passive-aggressive attitude I could muster that mom had about had an aneurysm the half dozen times she'd pounded into my skull that we had to be on the road by 7:15 that morning. My stepdad then did what any good spouse of twenty-five years would do, he defended her and said she'd told him she wanted to leave by 7:30.

I knew that wasn't true and that even if it had been, it was now after 7:45, so Kathy was late no matter which version of the truth we were accepting as real. I tried to laugh it off by calling him out on it and said something like, "C'mon, you know she wanted to leave by 7:15. She's been saying it all week."

I thought we were now two grown men who could have an honest laugh about a situation we'd both been in a million times before.

I was wrong.

My words didn't sit well with Poppa Steve, and he let me know it! On the one hand, I think that's really cool, and I totally admire him for doing so. My mom is his wife, and he ALWAYS has her back. But if that was all that had been going on in that moment, I wouldn't be telling this story. Like all families, our issues are much more complex. This early morning on a couch in my childhood home was no different.

"You don't know what time your mom told me, AJ, so don't tell me what time she told me she wanted to leave!"

Poppa Steve gets loud when he's defending his wife or when he's trying to assert his authority and shut shit down. In this moment, both were happening simultaneously.

I was watching a lion protect his lioness, and my roar suddenly turned to more of a purrrrr.

Remember that scene in *The Lion King* where Simba is trying to ROAR like his dad Mufasa, but lets out the cutest little noise instead? In this moment, I felt like young Simba, except there was nothing "cute" about this moment. I was frustrated, he was frustrated, and Kathy was still packing her socks, I assume.

On the surface, this entire story may sound so simple. Kathy wanted to get on the road, AJ called her out for being late, and Steve defended his wife to her prick son. Anyone who's ever lived knows that family dynamics are never that simple.

This story is actually about triangulation and why we should avoid this common relational pitfall at ALL COSTS!

I was frustrated with my mom, and truth be told, I'm sure he was, too, but instead of taking my concern directly to her or keeping it to myself, I complained to my stepdad and did so in front of my baby sister Kenz, neither of which was a good idea. He's endured a lifetime of waiting on the love of his life, but he would never articulate that to me or my sister; he'd only bring that up directly to her. Initially, this encounter really frustrated me, which is why I've waited over six months to revisit this story.

I started writing this chapter in October; it's now May. This story illustrates a common family dynamic that I felt compelled to explore, but I couldn't figure out quite how to do that until last night.

I finally broke down and allowed Emile to start reading the rough draft of my manuscript. That wasn't an easy decision to make, because I'm a perfectionist, and I don't like sharing anything until it's just right, but it was certainly the right decision. For six years he has witnessed firsthand the dynamics my family had established decades before he came into the picture. I'm sure that has been overwhelming for him at times, but he's a pretty incredible human being, and not only has he adapted, he has paid very close attention.

Initially, this chapter was about my personal frustrations with my parents and in particular, with my mom. The problem with taking that approach is that it wasn't an honest representation of her or of my deep love for her. Emile picked up on that the moment he read the chapter.

"I love you, and I understand what you think you're trying to say with this chapter, but for me, it doesn't match the flow of the book. Also, I know you don't want to hurt your mom, and the way this chapter reads right now, I'm afraid it might do that. I don't want you to use this book as an attempt to 'save' your mom, AJ. She has her flaws, we all do, but she's almost sixty, and she is who she is. I know how much you love who she is, so focus on that, and find a way to tell THAT story in a way that will benefit your readers."

Good God, did he hit the nail on the head! I'd been racking my brain trying to figure out how to tell the story of my relationship with my mom in a way that both illustrates our roadblocks, as well as makes it crystal clear that she is my best friend on the planet (sorry, Emile).

So now I'm sitting on our couch looking up at my boyfriend in complete awe as he perfectly articulates what I've spent half a year trying to figure out.

"I just want readers to know how much I love my mom, but also how much it hurts to know that she can't say the things to me that my heart needs to hear when it comes to difficult issues with my sister Kari. One of the people I love more than anyone on the planet hurt me so deeply the day she judged my sexuality, and the person I would talk to about that, my person, is my mom, but she can't be my person on this because the person who gutted me is her daughter. How do I tell THAT story?"

Emile: "Just like that. Put into your book everything you just said to me. You want to help your readers; THAT will help them. Don't hold back, AJ, but always come from a place of love."

I'm so going to marry that guy!

"Okay, I can do that."

So this morning I woke up at 6:30 a.m. ready to put our messy family dynamics onto these pages and tackle one of my biggest personal roadblocks. I call this "The Triangle of Doom!"

Much as I did when I was complaining to my stepdad the morning of the Nashville trip, I've had a tendency in life to take my issues with someone to a third party in hopes that one of two things will happen.

One: They'll agree with me wholeheartedly and assure me that I'm 100 percent right and my feelings are valid.

OR

Two: They'll take what I've said back to the third party in the triangle and let them know what I was too afraid to share directly.

Each of these options feels good short-term, but neither builds the type of understanding and mutual respect necessary to maintain a healthy relationship.

As I came to this realization, it became abundantly clear that THIS same dynamic has played a major role in my conflict with Kari. On a surface level, I've always been aware that my sister, my mom, and I have mastered the art of triangulation, but I'd never explored how deeply that has impacted each of us. So let's go there.

When I had initially shared what my sister said to me that day outside of Lemonade with my mom, her response was swift and supportive. I needed that, and mom knew it, because she's awesome like that. Since then, it has felt like her level of support has ebbed and flowed. I know for a fact that my mom understands God has gifted me with the ability to communicate, but He has also challenged me by giving me obstacles to overcome in life in pursuit of my purpose. My sexuality has been one of those obstacles, but it's also a gift, one that I would not trade for anything in the world. My sexuality and the way others have used it to judge me and place labels on me have sent me on a journey that has nearly taken me over the edge countless times, but it has only made me stronger each time God has pulled me back from the brink.

My sexuality is the greatest blessing the Lord could have given me, but I've spent a lifetime being hurt by that gift so that I could know the pain necessary to build the compassion to show others how to use the same gift to spread love.

My sister doesn't share the same perspective.

That's okay. She's my sister and I love her, but only I know what has been placed on my heart, just like she is the only person who knows what's been placed on hers.

That conversation on the sidewalk changed my life. In some ways, I feel like I've lost my best friend, but on the flip side, it forced me to find myself. The journey has had its share of ups and downs.

Like I mentioned earlier, I facetime my mom just about every single day, and as I've struggled to make sense of this new reality between my sister and me, the conversation would always somehow turn to Kari. I'd either ask, because I'm always curious to know how she's doing, or mom would bring her up, because I know it breaks my mom's heart that our relationship has disintegrated to this point. Either way, the triangle kept rearing its ugly head.

"Your sister is moving to Texas with her husband to study and build their ministry."

"Cool, I hope that works out for them."

I would play it cool and try to keep the conversation moving, but that rarely worked.

"Sorry, mom, but what do you mean she's moving to Texas? Where's she going to live? What's she going to do for work? Do you know the church they're getting involved with? Are they the good kind of Christians or the other kind?"

I think what I really wanted to know but was afraid to ask was this, "Are they the type of Christians who are going to further convince her that her brother is going to burn in the fiery pits of hell if he doesn't abandon his sexuality, or are they the compassionate type of Christians who know not to judge others—you know, LIKE CHRIST?"

I rarely go there because I'm not sure I want to know the answer.

I remember feeling frustrated, hurt, and oddly relieved at the very same time during this one particular conversation with my mom—the one I ACTUALLY had, not the one I was too afraid to have. Having lived with my sister in LA for nearly six years and now barely ever seeing her has been torture. In some weird way, it feels almost worse than a death. You know how people often say breakups are harder to deal with than a death, because the other person has *chosen* to no longer be in the relationship, whereas when someone passes away, it's usually not a result of a choice? Well, since getting married and changing her views on my lifestyle, my sister has chosen to distance herself from me, and as a means of survival, I've done the same.

It breaks my heart, and I'm not sure how to fix it. Just seeing these words in front of me right now is causing my skin to crawl and my tear ducts to go into overdrive. I hate where we are. My sister means everything to me, and I'm not sure how to process our new reality, but I do know that a healthy first step is to break "The Triangle of Doom."

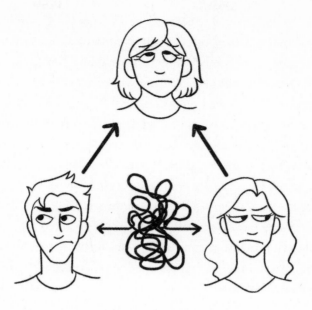

So, I'm trying.

Lately, I try not bringing our issues up when I speak to my mom, and on the odd chance that Kari and I have a conversation, I try to only ask about her and hope that she's curious to know how I've been doing. Currently, it feels like we're in a bit of a holding pattern. I think we might stay in this place for the time being.

We've both hurt each other many times and caused our mom a lot of pain along the way, but we're now thirty-three and thirty-seven years old, so it's up to us to resolve our issues as adults. I'm not sure I'm ready to let go of the pain, and I can't see just how I would even do that, but I'm trying. It still hurts me inside when I try seeking answers from my mom and she remains neutral, but that type of hurt is temporary. I know my mom wants our relationship to heal, so maybe this is her way of stepping back and allowing us to work through this so that we get it right once and for all. That's my dream; it always has been.

While our mom used to tell each of us what we wanted to hear because we're her babies and she just wanted each of us to be happy, this new version is much healthier. I think many parents have a really hard time letting their children work things out on their own, especially once those children become adults and the issues between them are no longer about who hit whom or who took the last popsicle from the freezer and didn't share. It's not easy for parents to step back and allow their children to handle issues as adults, because for decades, mom and dad were the solution to every problem. That's not the case anymore, and my mom sees that now, which sometimes hurts because I want her to fix this broken relationship, but ultimately, it makes me proud because it shows that she believes in our ability to handle our issues as adults. I credit her renewed relationship with God.

We were raised Catholic, but after my sister and I were each confirmed at age sixteen, our family really stopped attending church regularly. We had lost a few family members in a short period of time, and I think that pushed us all further from faith at a time when we should've been leaning in. Also, at the time, the Catholic Church was struggling to fight off abuse scandals left and right, so it didn't feel like a place we could call home.

Slowly but surely, through a series of nudges from the universe, each of us did find our way back home. First myself, and then my sister, and finally our mom. We each have very different relationships with faith, but each is beautiful in its own way, and as we each strengthen our two-way communication with the big guy upstairs, it's infinitely easier to avoid triangulation with each other.

Also, for many years I never thought any of us would ever set foot inside a church again. We actually used to joke while attending weddings that it was a good sign that the church didn't go up in flames with us in the building. Yet here we are, three individuals of deep faith with profound love for God and for one another, trying desperately to rebuild individual relationships with each other after decades operating in "The Triangle of Doom."

I'm not sure where this journey will take us or how my relationship with Kari will be restored, but I find comfort in knowing that there's hope for us. If the three of us can go to church again every Sunday morning, ANYTHING is possible.

Script Rewrites

This one is very simple but will have a profound impact on your life. Go to the store or jump on Amazon and order a pack of thank-you cards. Choose one person for whom you feel love, but with whom you always seem to butt heads. Try to pick someone you've found yourself with in your own "Triangle of Doom," and consider how reaching out to that person directly might improve your line of communication and break a pattern of unhealthy triangulation. Maybe you're in a good place with this person right now, or maybe you're not speaking at all. Maybe this person has been a part of your life either forever or for just a short period of time. Regardless, I want this person to be someone you care about and with whom you have a relationship that you would like to improve.

Now, grab one of those cards and write this person a thank-you note. Thank them for every wonderful memory you've ever shared, every bit of sound advice they've ever given you, and every kind thing they've ever done for you. Don't hold back. I want you to show this person how much he or she means to you. It's important that this is in written form, because it will be something they can glance back at time and time again to remind them of the kindness of your words.

Do not mention any negative memories, and don't air any dirty laundry or gripes you may have with this person, simply show them gratitude. When you're happy with your note, put a stamp on it (those sticky things that make mail go places) and drop it in the mailbox. Then, release ALL expectations.

This exercise is for YOU. By sharing your heart with others, you are doing your part. How they respond is in no way a reflection of you.

You may feel the need to ask them if they've received your note or further elaborate once they've received your message, but resist these urges. Let your written words speak for themselves. Your words are powerful, let them do the work. If the recipient of your note wants to engage, that's great, but that is not the goal of this exercise.

The beauty in this simple exercise is that there is no wrong outcome. The recipient of your act of kindness may respond with love and gratitude, opening your relationship up to new possibilities of connection and deeper communication, which is a beautiful thing. Or this person may never acknowledge your act of kindness, which is also okay. The point is that you sent out love, you were authentic, and you were vulnerable. You can only control your actions in the world, and as long as you are acting from a place of love, that love will always come back to you, maybe not in the form of a thank-you note or an improved relationship with the person to whom your kindness was directed, but in ways you might never have considered.

Also, it feels awesome to spread love in the form of a handwritten note, so it's good for your soul. Every few weeks, I send out a couple thank-you cards to people in my life whom I care about, and each time, my soul feels a little fuller. That is my hope for you, my friend.

I think I'll write my mom a thank-you note right now. Maybe my sister, too.

CHAPTER THIRTEEN:

DARING AF

Scene 26: *A Chorus Line* & A Motorola RAZR

INT. HARLEM APARTMENT - BATHROOM - NIGHT

Water spurts out from the nozzle of a showerhead. A MAN'S blurred figure is behind the glass of the shower door. Steam rolls out over the top of the shower and fills the Pepto-Bismol pink bathroom, fogging the mirror.

INT. HARLEM APARTMENT — BEDROOM — NIGHT

AJ sits on his bed, ready for a relaxing evening after a long day of waiting tables.

He reaches for the TV remote on his nightstand and notices a flashing light. It's coming from his boyfriend JIMMY's Motorola RAZR flip phone, charging next to the remote.

AJ looks toward the phone, then at the bathroom, then back to the phone. He reaches for the phone.

He picks up the phone tentatively, opens it, and his jaw drops.

I stormed in on Jimmy mid-shower with his phone in my hand. He was getting ready to head to his job as a barback at Barracuda, an iconic gay bar in Chelsea. The moment I saw what was on his phone, his getting to work on time became the least of my worries.

"I miss you in my bed! I miss you in my bed, Jimmy! Who the fuck is texting you that they miss you in their bed?"

"What? What are you talking about, AJ?"

"This, Jimmy! Why is some guy texting you these words along with THIS picture?"

"Oh, it's just a joke. He's being stupid!"

Was my boyfriend of four years really trying to pass this off as a silly joke?

"Jimmy, I don't think it's funny that some random dude is texting MY boyfriend a picture of his dick, telling him how badly he misses having you in his bed. I don't find that funny AT ALL!"

I was beyond livid.

Jimmy acted like it was no big deal, shut down the conversation, and headed to Barracuda. That night was the beginning of the end for us.

The year was 2007, the setting was New York City, and the love of my life was sleeping with the lead actor from the Broadway revival of *A Chorus Line*. I should've known it wasn't the best idea to convince my college sweetheart to move to the Big Apple to watch me pursue my dreams, especially considering that he was more than content teaching toe-touches and double-fulls to teenage girls back in Columbus, Ohio. He was an elite cheerleading coach, and he was phenomenal at it. People do crazy things for love. We were two people doing crazy things, and we were very much in love, but also, we were in our mid-twenties, so we clearly had life figured out and would find a way to make it work, until we didn't.

Also, the cheating devastated me and made me feel like the least attractive, least lovable guy on the planet. I listened to A LOT of Ne-Yo back then to get me through it. What I did not listen to was Broadway music, especially the soundtrack to *A Chorus Line*.

Which brings me to the boy in the tights from, you guessed it, *A Chorus Line*.

I call him "the boy" for a few reasons.

First, I don't remember his name.

Second, an actual man would never disrespect themselves or another relationship by sending a tacky dick pic like that. That's the type of stuff BOYS do.

Third, I feel like being petty. This was my first real heartbreak, and while I've been over it for a decade, writing about it after all these years still stirs up uncomfortable emotions from a time when I felt broken.

Jimmy and I were sharing a tiny apartment in Harlem with a guy we'd been introduced to by my friend JR, who had also gotten Jimmy the job at Barracuda. It was a cramped space, there was rarely a moment of silence, and our entire building always smelled like curry. Jimmy hated curry.

We'd been New Yorkers for about six months when our already dicey communication began to break down even further. My gut told me something was off. He was working late most nights and not coming home until 7 a.m. some mornings, and that just didn't sit well with me. Jimmy had always been a drinker, and having grown up with an alcoholic father, I was always hyper-aware of my partner's drinking habits.

To be clear, I've never been the type of guy who checks cell phones, but something inside of me told me to check his. The picture quality wasn't the best, but the moderately sized penis accompanied by the words, "I miss you in my bed" were crystal clear! I'll never forget those words.

I felt gutted. I felt stupid. And we were too broke to live separately, so we continued sharing the same apartment for weeks after RAZR-gate.

While this was all going down, I had one place of refuge and that was the restaurant where I was working. I was a server at a French brasserie / sushi bar, whatever the eff that is, a block away from Carnegie Hall, and my coworkers there were pretty awesome. They may not have been dear friends of mine, but they were all that

I had and a much-welcomed distraction. It was early spring, April I believe, and the city was coming back to life after a miserably brutal winter. The restaurant started opening its large doors to create an open-air feel, and the outdoor seating was coming out of storage. Like most restaurants in the city, that meant tables and chairs on a noisy, smelly sidewalk, but I loved working outdoors. Although I was probably inhaling toxic fumes every time I greeted a table, I was outdoors, and that felt like the right place to be. I'd spent enough time crying to myself alone in my apartment. Slowly but surely, my personality started to return, my heart started to heal, and my swagger was once again in full effect. I had no idea how I was going to get past this heartbreak, but I was certain I would survive it. Unfortunately, NYC public transportation had a different plan for me.

As I'm taking my 4,092nd steak frites and rainbow roll order one night (it's actually an oddly satisfying pairing), I look up and what do I see? The boy! Yes, THAT boy, the one with the moderately sized penis. Where, you wonder? Oh, just on the side of a massive city bus, showcased front and center on an advertisement for *A Chorus Line*! And adding insult to injury, the guy was the freakin' lead, and he admittedly looked really good in his gold leotard, although they had OBVIOUSLY stuffed his crotch region or bulked it up in Photoshop, because I knew better.

Now, nowhere was safe. In my apartment, I was left alone with my thoughts. At work, I could get stuck serving tables on the sidewalk and be faced with this absurdly inaccurate gold penis in my face over and over again because of course, the bus ran in front of the restaurant every ten minutes or so, and apparently, the marketing budget for a Broadway show is much larger than the moderately sized penis I'd seen on that flip phone. Have I made it clear yet how NOT impressive his penis was? Because I really want to make sure to get that point across. I'm not bitter, I've moved on, I swear. But seriously, though, it wasn't anything to write home about.

But he was on a bus promoting an amazing accomplishment, and I was left refilling the San Pellegrinos of European tourists on a trash laden sidewalk in Manhattan. I knew that I could do better.

So I decided to call up my sister Kari and revisit a promise we'd made to each other years earlier but had never followed through on. As children, we'd said someday we were going to move to Los Angeles and make it big, whatever that meant. She was about to graduate college the following month, so now seemed like the perfect opportunity to take the leap together. Also, I was really lonely and missed her a lot. The only problem was that I still had four months left on my lease, and there was no way I was getting out of it. So, I convinced her to move in with me for the summer.

To be honest, in my seemingly eternal state of despair, I'm not really sure I'd thought this one through, because the day she moved in, I realized how crammed our summer was about to be. She didn't bring much with her, just one suitcase of normal human belongings and one full of bikinis. No joke, she was a bikini model for Hawaiian Tropic at the time and had brought an entire piece of luggage full of swimwear. My sister is one of the most gorgeous women I've ever seen, and I wasn't the only person to think so. One night, while attending school on a full ride volleyball scholarship to Carson Newman College in Jefferson City, Tennessee, my sister had entered a contest at a bar—and won. She spent her senior year and the months after traveling the world and shooting bikini campaigns for the most famous sunscreen makers on the planet. She accumulated a lot of bikinis along the way, and her luggage was bursting at the seams with this collection! It was actually overweight at the airport, and she had to switch five pounds' worth over to her carry-on, if that gives you an indication of how many swimsuits she'd packed for a summer in a city that was at least an hour train ride from the nearest beach.

I had plenty of storage space, especially since her two-pieces didn't really take up that much room, but I hadn't come up with a game plan for HER. My living room, kitchen, and dining room were one and the same, so that was not a sleeping option for her. I had a couch in my bedroom, but it just didn't feel right to stick my sis on that for the summer, and I was not about to sleep there. So, we decided to share a bed.

I was a newly single young man in my prime, living in the most exciting city on the planet—and my nights were spent sleeping next to my baby sister. It sounds weird, but it was a perfect summer after we worked out one major kink. On the first night, I woke up at some point and found that we were literally intertwined. Spooning is for rookies. My sister and I were sleeping in a full-on embrace!

She'd also just gotten out of a relationship with a guy who didn't understand the word loyalty either, so we were both recovering from being cheated on and adjusting to the cuddle-free life, and neither of us was succeeding, apparently. I love my sister, but that was NEVER happening again. I bought a body pillow the next day, and we never crossed that fluffy midline ever again. We made a lot of memories that summer but never forgot our goal of one day making it to Los Angeles. As the end of my lease approached, we decided to take the leap!

I'd never been to the West Coast, but my sister had just filmed a cross-country road trip that had aired on NBC as a Saturday afternoon TV special, and she'd made a new friend who helped convince her that LA was the place to be. So we decided to fulfill our childhood promise to each other and head to Los Angeles on the advice of Kato Kaelin. (Yes, THAT Kato Kaelin. If you don't know who he, Google "OJ Simpson Kato Kaelin" and enjoy your trip down the rabbit hole. My sister and I were inspired to move to Los Angeles by a man who was at the center of the "Trial of the Century!" How random is that?) Kari and I rented a white Ford Bronco, and off we went. (I'm totally kidding, but I knew you were thinking it!)

Again, if that reference just flew right over your head, get to Googling and I'll be here waiting for your return. No judgment, I promise.

Ok great, glad to have you back!

Like so many people, moving to LA was a dream we'd had for many years, but it had been one we'd never had the courage to act on. So we were filled with both excitement and pure terror. Making the move to New York was a big deal, but at least we were still in the same time zone as our family and friends in Ohio. If my life fell apart, home was only a quick flight away. California might as well have been on Mars, because from the moment we actually decided to make the move, it felt like a world away.

I made a conscious decision to not let the experience overwhelm me because I knew if I allowed my fears in, I'd never make it to California or my destiny. My gut told me to take the trip in bits and pieces so that I wouldn't feel consumed by the enormity of the decision we'd made.

When I give talks, I often speak of the importance of breaking large goals down into smaller, more workable chunks to avoid getting overwhelmed. Breaking down our cross-country trip was exactly what we were about to do as we made our way from New York to Los Angeles; we were not going to let the adventure overwhelm us. With Jimmy and the heartbreak he'd brought into my life slowly fading away in my rearview mirror, I was finally ready to focus on the road ahead, and my sister was right there by my side for the journey.

What could possibly go wrong?

Script Rewrites

Life can feel overwhelming at times, especially when we are challenging ourselves to achieve big goals. The next time you set out to accomplish something that feels too big for you, make a mental note of what exactly is stirring up the fear inside of you.

Once you've acknowledged that, ask yourself what one thing you can do right now to get you closer to your goal. Instead of trying to go from A to Z, focus on getting from A to B. If you can do that enough times, you'll build positive momentum toward your goal, and before you know it, you'll be standing at Z, ready to dream up a brand-new goal!

CHAPTER FOURTEEN:

ANGELENO AF

Scene 33: AJ Moves to Tinseltown!

INT. BLACK CHEVROLET EQUINOX — NIGHT

AJ is at the wheel, driving down a long, lonely highway with KARI asleep in the passenger seat, her head resting gently against the window.

Her SOFT SNORE fills the SUV.

As he continues down the highway, the light from each streetlamp he passes cascades across AJ's face through the window.

The car is packed to the brim with clothing and furniture, with hangers and lampshades popping out from the mass.

AJ's stomach starts to GRUMBLE. He puts a hand to it as a look of concern crosses his face.

AJ's eyes follow an approaching lodging sign. The headlight illuminates the words ECONO LODGE.

AJ takes a right off the highway.

"Kari, wake up, I'm legit about to shit my pants!"

"Huh? Where are we? Why did you pull off the highway?"

My sister had been fast asleep for much of the past two days as we drove cross-country, pulling a six by twelve foot U-Haul trailer behind my 2005 Chevy Equinox. I was barely comfortable driving my new car, and as much as I would've loved for her to take the wheel for a bit, I knew I'd be a nervous wreck either way, so it was probably for the best that I continue at the helm.

"I said I'm about to shit my pants! I talked to mom earlier, and she said if we got too tired that she would pay for us to pull over and get a hotel room for the night, and this is the only lodging I've seen for a mile."

"We're going to stay at an Econo Lodge?"

We both laughed.

It was just before midnight, and the motel barely looked like it was functioning, but all I needed was a place to rest my head, and more immediately, a place to rest my tushy!

We found a place to park and walked up to the entrance, with me doing my best impression of a penguin as I fought to keep my dignity intact. I was sure that the lobby would have a restroom for me to use while my sister checked us in.

I was wrong.

As the front desk employee informed us that there was no restroom available, panic started taking over.

"Okay, that's fine, we'll just check in and I'll use the restroom in our room, it's no big deal."

I was lying, it was a HUGE deal!

Next, we were told that we had to wait a couple of minutes because the register needed to be switched out at midnight, and we couldn't check in until that was complete.

"Excuse me? Why can't you check us in right now? It's 11:58, we've got time!" I couldn't believe the absurdity of this moment.

"I'm sorry, sir, but it'll be just a few more minutes."

"I DON'T HAVE A FEW MORE MINUTES!" was what was running through my mind. On the outside I was calm; inside I was losing my damn mind and about to lose much more right down my pant leg!

I fought through the waves of pressure, followed by cramps and then relief, wondering which wave would be the one to finally take me out. I'd dealt with these sorts of stomach issues in the past, but never in the lobby of a low-grade motel in Albuquerque, New Mexico, before.

Finally, we were given our room key, and off we went.

This was a motel, so there were no elevators, and we had conveniently been given a room on the second floor at the other end of the complex.

Awesome.

We got to our room just in the nick of time. I placed the key card in the door and the light flashed RED.

"NOOOOOOOOO!!! Oh my God, Kari, I'm not kidding, I really am going to shit my pants! I can't make it back down to the lobby to get a new key!"

"It's okay, I'll do it. You just wait right here."

She was laughing. I was not.

"Please, run!"

I slid down the door and sat on the concrete facing the parking lot, praying that my sister would make it back to me in record time.

"I'm coming. Hang in there, brother!"

"Aaaaahhhh that was quick! Thank you, sis. Now, please open the door!"

She swiped the key card. STILL FUCKING RED!

"Are you serious?!? How on earth can they not figure out how to give us a working room key!?"

With my cheeks pressed tightly together and my breathing sounding more like that of a woman in labor than a twenty-five-year-old aspiring actor moving cross-country to chase his dreams in LA, I decided that I could not take the chance that my sister would return a third time with a faulty key.

So, I stood and headed for the pool area. We'd passed it on our way to our room, and I thought there might be a bathroom there that I could use. It was also next to the laundry facility, and even though it was now past midnight, I was in desperate need of relief and not thinking clearly.

I made it to the pool area, but there was no bathroom. I knew another trip up the stairs was not in the cards for me, so I did what I had to do. I popped a squat...IN THE SHRUBBERY SURROUNDING THE ECONO LODGE POOL!!!

This was not how I had seen this trip going! We were moving to Los Angeles to chase our destiny and find fame. As I relieved myself among some low-level bushes, not even able to find an available bathroom, I thought maybe I was in way over my head. I was humiliated.

It got worse.

As I was squatting, pooping, and questioning my life choices, a mother and her young child walked past. Mortified, I smiled awkwardly as she pulled her child closer, covered his eyes, and scurried along! I dug through the mulch for the largest, smoothest piece I could find, cleaned myself as well as I could, and ran up to our room, hoping the woman hadn't called security on me, which she would've had every right to do.

I had just taken a shit in a bush. PUBLICLY!!!

I got back to our room, where Kari was resting peacefully on her bed, waiting for me to rush in to use the toilet.

"Where'd you go? I thought you had to poop?"

"Oh, I did, but I took care of it," I said, still not believing what I'd just done.

I told her what had just happened. We laughed until it hurt and happy tears filled our eyes. Maybe driving cross-country for two days straight while chugging Red Bulls and eating junk food hadn't been the best idea, but it sure made for one hell of a story! My sister and were on our own, and if we could get through this with a laugh, we were going to be just fine in LA.

"Oh, my God, AJ! You have to tell this story someday when you get famous. It's just too good!"

I don't know that I'm famous, but it is a pretty funny story and the perfect beginning to our time out west. I'd always been told I was full of shit, now the bushes at an Econo Lodge in Albuquerque, New Mexico, were, too!

The next morning, we gathered our belongings and continued on our journey, still recovering from the absurdity of the night before. We had only been able to get four or five hours of sleep, because we had a thirteen-hour drive ahead of us and needed to pick up the keys to our new apartment from the leasing office in North Hollywood, California, before 7 p.m. So before the sun was up, we were back on the road.

I remember listening to Kanye West's "Graduation" album on repeat those few days we spent together in my Chevy Equinox, and those songs still bring me back to that moment in our lives every time I hear them. Kari and I were embarking on the adventure of a lifetime, and we were ready to take Hollywood by storm!

About twelve hours later, we found ourselves in the middle of our first rush hour experience.

It was absolutely TERRIFYING!

Keep in mind, we were exhausted, both physically and mentally. We were doing something no one we knew had ever done. There's no such thing as rush hour in Celina, Ohio, and we felt in over our heads once again. Being the older brother, I did what I've always done. I acted like I had my shit together so that my sister wouldn't be scared. I was terrified inside and found myself clutching that steering wheel for dear life. At moments, the traffic was at a standstill, which I actually preferred, but then it would pick up unexpectedly, and I would imagine I was actually my namesake, AJ Foyt, speeding my way through the Indy 500, but with a couple of major differences. I wasn't THAT AJ, I was hauling a trailer for the first time in my life, and we were in the mountains!

I knew that North Hollywood was in what's called "the Valley," but I guess I'd never really considered what that actually meant, because the mountains really caught me off guard. Ohio is pretty flat; I was not prepared for this. More self-doubt started to creep into my mind.

Eventually, we did make it to our apartment complex. Just minutes before the deadline, we found room on the street to park our SUV and trailer. I remember expecting the leasing office employee to greet us with open arms and big congratulations on making the move to LA; maybe there would even be balloons involved, or a bottle of complimentary champagne.

Nope.

She handed us the keys and told us to take the elevator to the second floor and turn left, and then she was off. We were on our own.

I had one friend living in LA at the time, and he was waiting for us the moment we picked up our keys and were ready to start unpacking. He had ordered a Domino's pizza and brought over a twelve-pack of beer to welcome us. We'd been roommates years before while attending THE Ohio State University, so I was grateful to have him there that first night.

Midwesterners know how to greet a newcomer.

Before the leasing office employee had left for the night, we'd asked where we could park our SUV and trailer overnight. The U-Haul drop-off location was just down the street but wouldn't be open again until the next morning. She'd said we could park it in our tandem spots in the parking garage, and she went on her merry way.

We did some unpacking, had a few beers, and ate some pizza. Kari found an empty shopping cart on the sidewalk and had the brilliant idea to use it to help carry our stuff upstairs. We were a little tipsy as well as very tired and ready to go to bed, so this seemed like the perfect way to speed the process up. The three of us had so much fun unpacking that night! The world was at our fingertips, and this was just the beginning of what would become an incredible season in our lives.

We finished unloading the trailer and went to park in the tandem spots we'd been assigned. What we hadn't been told was that the parking spots were in a garage located UNDER our apartment complex. Mildly inebriated and beyond exhausted, we were certain the trailer would fit through the security gate.

It did not.

So about halfway down the ramp into the garage, we heard the pipes overhead scraping the top of the trailer and knew we were in trouble. We all panicked; I'm pretty sure I wanted to cry, and we just stared at each other for a moment. Again, in over our heads!

My buddy Joe hopped out of the car and started directing me as I attempted to back this massive trailer up the steep ramp we'd just driven down. A simple bathroom break at an Econo Lodge had proven to be anything but simple, and now driving backward up a short ramp was making an already exhausting twenty-four hours feel impossible. But, again, I did not want my sister to see me scared. I'd agreed to go on this journey with her, but I was feeling overwhelmed and ill-prepared.

For the next hour, Joe guided me as I inched slowly up that ramp. Eventually, we were clear, and we all took a deep sigh of relief.

"Oh, my God, that was awful! I really thought we were going to be stuck down there forever, you guys! Now, where are we going to park this thing?"

We had yet one more hurdle to overcome. Street parking in LA is notoriously difficult, that much we did know. We drove around the corner and were shocked to find space for both the Equinox and the trailer. Finally, something was going right!

We parked the car, walked up to our apartment, and fell asleep. We were officially Angelenos!

Joe had also gotten us donuts for the following morning because he's awesome like that, so I grabbed one and headed out the door to return the U-Haul trailer. But as I got to my car, not only was there a parking ticket under my windshield wiper, but my car had been egged!

"What the fuck?! Who on earth would egg my new car on my first night here? Aaaahhhh!"

I was not a happy camper. Again, was the universe telling me that I'd made a huge mistake and that I was in over my head?

I grabbed my parking ticket, got in my car, and headed to the U-Haul drop-off, thinking to myself, "NOW I'm an Angeleno!"

Script Rewrites

Life isn't easy, and big changes are often accompanied by big obstacles. In the moment, I allowed those obstacles to contribute to self-doubt in me, and I questioned my decision to move to LA. Looking back, I see those same obstacles as having been opportunities to prove to God how badly I wanted the things I was seeking. Oftentimes, a simple shift in perspective is all we need in order to view hardships as blessings. What blessings have you been blocking because you've been too busy complaining to see the opportunities for growth that are in front of you each and every day?

Make a list of roadblocks you've experienced that have turned out to be blessings in disguise. Refer to this list the next time you think you've hit another roadblock or rock bottom moment, and consider what lessons the universe might be trying to teach you. If you stay open to possibilities for growth, I think you'll be pleasantly surprised.

CHAPTER FIFTEEN:

PERSEVERANT AF

Scene 45: AJ's Big Break

EXT. SAHARA DESERT - DAY

Knees come crashing down into golden sand, spraying it into the air. Hands follow as they frantically pull away the course stuff.

The boiling sun beats down on the bare necks of three FIGURES toiling in the desert: AJ, Kari, and Ryan (AJ's ex-boyfriend).

Sweat pools from their foreheads and darkens the shirt on their backs. Their BREATHING is shallow as it gets lost in the Sahara wind.

Kari and Ryan break from their work.

Ryan SCOFFS as he watches AJ continue.

> RYAN
>
> What are you doing? We're not going to find water in the middle of the desert.

> KARI
>
> Yeah, how is that even possible?

> AJ
>
> Just shut up and dig!

We were just hours into Day One of a month-long expedition, and my teammates were already driving me nuts. To be fair, my teammates were bikini model (and my younger sister) Kari and my ex-boyfriend Ryan, who had just cheated on me with our best friend a couple of months prior, so my patience level had started out quite low to begin with.

"What do you think you're going to find down there, AJ? A magic well?"

Ryan had always been a bit of a smartass.

"Yeah, like water is just going to magically appear," my sister said. She clearly didn't understand the clue: "Find water for your camels in the ancient Berber way."

We were smack-dab in the middle of the Sahara desert, trying to fill large glass jugs with water that we weren't quite sure even existed. Luckily, I'd remembered learning about water being a few feet below the surface in desert conditions and was willing to trust my gut—my teammates, not so much.

"You guys, will you please stop standing there with your hands on your hips and help me dig?"

I was hot, I was exhausted, and I was frustrated. We'd just spent a solid three or four hours climbing up a sand dune followed by an hours long trek across the desert via camel, all of this under a scorching sun and in temperatures over 110 degrees. This was the opportunity of a lifetime, and my teammates were throwing in the towel on Day One. That's just not how I roll.

As I continued to dig, now receiving "help" from other teams who hadn't come up with a plan of their own, something inside of me said to just keep going. I could either stop and let doubt start to creep in or I could double down and trust my gut. I've always been a fan of betting on myself, so I doubled down.

It paid off.

"Oh my God, there's water!" my new buddy/competitor Akbar yelled out in disbelief as muddy water started filling the hole we'd spent the past twenty minutes digging.

"You've figured it out! That's brilliant," the show's creator and executive producer, the legendary Mark Burnett, exclaimed.

Just a couple of feet to my right and just off camera, Mark wanted to be there to see the show he'd dreamed up LIVE in action! As a diehard fan of *Survivor*, another one of his creations, he'd been an idol of mine for over a decade, and now he was two feet away watching me solve a challenge that he'd created.

Imagine having the opportunity to do something totally awesome in front of one of your idols in the middle of a foreign country, surrounded by cameras, knowing that it would all air on ABC in front of millions of viewers. The experience was surreal!

I'd spent my childhood dreaming of the day when I would get the opportunity to show the world what I was capable of, and as I filled our team's jug, I realized THIS was that day, the one I'd been dreaming of. That's a pretty wild realization to come to and not one you get to experience too many times in life, so I was determined to take full advantage.

Kari and Ryan casually riding camels through Morocco, while I'm being rescued by a helpful crewmember in disguise.

Our team, named Fab 3 by the show's producers, completed the two-day opening leg of the competition in second place, and I was personally overwhelmed by this accomplishment. We were up against former pro athletes, police officers, firefighters, and even a team of outdoor adventurers, yet had somehow found a way to finish in second place. None of us had ever even been camping before, yet here we were thriving in the wild.

THAT was wild!

As we came across the finish line of stage one, having spent a solid fourteen hours on the course that day, trekking through the desert, rappelling down cliffs, and hiking up mountains, we were all overcome with a deep pride. For me, that resulted in ugly tears and a never-ending flow of snot.

Our producer, the one who'd been assigned to our team, pulled me aside immediately after host Dave Salmoni congratulated us on our accomplishment and directed us to our tent. As I looked just off camera and saw the entire crew cheering us on silently, many of them sobbing, I knew this was the opportunity of a lifetime and the start of something special.

I cried all the way through that first interview. In the real world, that would make me look like a crazy person, but we weren't in the real world; we were in TV world. In TV world, sobbing uncontrollably made me look vulnerable and would endear me to viewers. I was well aware of that.

Finally, I'd found a space where I could be my authentic, messy self and be rewarded for it!

Back in LA, the acting thing hadn't really been working out for me. I'd realized I had never really felt passionate about the craft, but still enjoyed being in front of people very much. I was having a problem figuring out how to make that happen, though, because I was looking at my opportunities through such a narrow lens. I'd never considered that I could just be ME until I spent that month in Morocco.

Mark Burnett had to leave after the first couple legs of the competition because he was also in the process of launching another brand-new show back in the states and needed to go convince one of its stars that the show would be a good move for her career. That star was Christina Aguilera and the show was...*The Voice*!

So, without my idol off camera cheering me on, I looked inwards, and for the first time in my life, I trusted my instincts completely. I felt a level of connection to the earth I'd never experienced. Being cut off from all technology and the outside world for an entire month was without a doubt one of the single most profound experiences of my life. Through that experience, I was able to get quiet, figure out who I truly was, and see what I was capable of when given the opportunity.

We didn't win *Expedition Impossible*, but we were one of only three teams to complete it. My sister Kari was the only woman to finish the competition; I told you she was a phenomenal athlete!

Crossing the finish line of *Expedition Impossible*, holding my sister Kari's hand, is still one of the proudest moments of my life.

Back in LA and adjusting to life in a first-world country again, I sought to find deeper meaning at every turn. I started reading every self-help book I could find: *The Alchemist, The Celestine Prophecy, The Secret*...I read them all! I wanted so desperately to feel that level of connection that I'd experienced in nature, but that I felt slowly slipping away as each day home passed.

Also a lover of the outdoors, Mark Burnett must've seen something in the Fab 3 because he asked us to come in before our show even began airing to discuss creating a reality series revolving around our lives and the interesting dynamics of our relationships with one another. We had a few developmental meetings and thought we were on our way, but then that "other" new show became a massive success, and we were pushed to the backburner. *The Voice* was a ratings juggernaut and a huge success for Mark Burnett, so we were no longer a priority. It made perfect sense, but it still stung.

During our last meeting with his team, one of Burnett's associates told me that Mark and the rest of the associates saw something special in me and encouraged me to develop it. It was suggested to me that I check out some TV hosting classes and see what I thought. So that's exactly what I did!

Life rarely works out as we expect, but my life was finally moving again, and I was thrilled about it!

So, I started studying with my first mentor, Maureen Browne. This was also where I would meet my future *Hollywood Today Live* co-host and work wife Kristen Brockman. She would later get me the opportunity at HTL, and I never would have met her had I not taken Mark's advice and signed up for that hosting class. The universe has a funny way of bringing people and opportunities into our lives once we start stepping out of our comfort zone.

From there, I was connected with a guy named Phil Svitek, who was in charge of this new online after show network called AfterBuzz TV. It was created by TV host Maria Menounos and her then boyfriend, Keven Undergaro, and was a great place for aspiring hosts to learn the skills necessary to work as on-air talent. I spent a couple of years there, learning how to work with co-hosts, sharpening my interviewing skills, and getting a feel for what a life as a TV host might look like.

It was an unpaid gig, and the studio was located out in Encino, California, about a forty-five-minute drive from my apartment. I was still working as a bartender to pay the bills, but hosting was my passion. I was dead broke at the time, spending every dime I had on hosting classes and gas money to drive to Encino, but I was determined to learn all that I could. I remember driving there one night with the windows down, air conditioning broken, and an empty gas tank, wondering how I was going to make it back home with no money in my bank account.

I remember praying to God that He would find a way to make it all work. I was still sort of an atheist at that time, but willing to try anything. I was barely surviving, but knew in my gut that it would all pay off someday, somehow.

During that last summer at AfterBuzz TV, I was asked to fill in for the *America's Got Talent* after show. I'd never even watched the program, but I agreed to do it. I had no idea what to expect but had decided this would be a great opportunity to show my professionalism. As a TV host, you never know what you'll be asked to cover from day to day, so I needed to push myself and show that I was capable.

I showed up prepared for the show, but not prepared to meet the love of my life.

On the first night of the *America's Got Talent* after show, I met a quiet, closeted young kid from Atlanta, Georgia, and his name was Emile.

At first, he became like a little brother to me. He was really shy back then, but I could tell there was so much more to him than he was letting on. We became friends for the next few months and spent hours talking to each other after taping our after show together, and he even started taking classes with Maureen on my recommendation.

I'm pretty sure he just wanted to be around me more, but I was okay with it. I kind of wanted to be around him, too...pretty a lotta bit (an inside joke there just for Emile).

As my time at AfterBuzz TV came to an end, I received a message from Kristen Brockman via Facebook telling me about this exciting new digital network called BiteSize TV. She'd been working there for the past few months and wanted to get me in. I interviewed for the job five times over the next year, each time being promised I would start immediately.

I think their idea of "immediately" was a little skewed, because months would go by and I'd be brought in again, assured each time that this time would be different.

Finally, after completely giving up on the idea that I'd ever actually be hired, I WAS ACTUALLY HIRED!

This was my big break and the first time I'd ever been paid to appear on camera. I was making $50 per day; I'd made it! Okay, so I wasn't exactly rolling in the dough, but I was learning and getting opportunities that were priceless. It was here that I had the chance to set foot on my very first red carpet and it was a big one!

One day, while we were filming digital segments for *Hollywood Today* before it became the TV show *Hollywood Today Live*, a group of important looking people came to watch us do our thing. As I walked up to the stage that day, I remember seeing a young girl wearing a silk leopard print blouse and saying to her, "That top looks great on you. I hear animal print is in right now!"

I didn't really know if what I was saying was true, but I did think she looked great, and I love making people feel good about themselves. After we wrapped, one of my bosses pulled me aside and told me that the people watching us were from CBS and they would like very much to meet with me.

I was floored!

"Um, yeah, I can definitely meet with them! When would they like to get together?"

"Now," my boss replied, "they're waiting upstairs."

Okay, I wasn't ready for that response, but I'd been working toward this opportunity for the past two years, so saying no wasn't an option.

As I walked into the upstairs office and a room filled with CBS executives, who now made me much more nervous than when I'd thought they were just well-dressed randoms, I struggled to clear my throat and say something that made me seem like I wasn't in the wrong room, something that made me seem like I belonged.

"Hey, you're that girl from downstairs with the great blouse!"

What the fuck was I saying!

"Yes, that's my assistant, Geri, and she has great style!"

Oh, my God! This woman has an assistant? She MUST be important!

"AJ, this is Linda Bell Blue, executive producer of *Entertainment Tonight*," my boss said as he introduced me to this fancy woman who had her own assistant.

I definitely recognized the name, even if I'd had no idea before now what she looked like. Linda Bell Blue was an ICON in the world of entertainment news. She had been the EP at *Entertainment Tonight*, the most watched entertainment news show on the planet, for the past nineteen years, and I was meeting her! I could barely contain myself.

"AJ, how would you like to attend the Golden Globes as a special guest of *Entertainment Tonight*? I think you're a star, and I'd love to see how you handle yourself on a red carpet."

Ummm, did she know that the Golden Globes were right around the corner? We were meeting on a Thursday; the Golden Globes were THAT Sunday!

I said yes, because how could I ever say no, but I didn't own a tux or dress shoes and had never been on a red carpet in my life. My boss agreed to pay for everything I needed, and off I went, running around town frantically searching for a tux to fit my 6'5" frame. Five stores and $1,000 later, I found one, but it was now Friday, and it still needed to be tailored because I'm "uniquely" built, so that was another hurdle to overcome. After I found a tailor and got my company to pay an additional $200 to cover the alterations, I was on my way.

So far, these problems were very privileged problems to have, and I'm keenly aware of that fact. As the show day approached, the shit really started to hit the fan. All the self-doubt started to creep in, and it was crippling. I didn't believe I deserved the opportunity, and I certainly didn't feel that I was prepared for it. I'd spent years studying to become a better host and taken all sorts of free work as

I learned the craft. Reading from a teleprompter while interviewing a celebrity in the midst of total chaos, all while a producer is constantly barking commands in your earpiece, is no easy task, and up to this point, I'd only practiced it in class. At the Golden Globes, I would have the opportunity to see Nancy O'Dell do it live and in person, so long as I could make it there.

I was driving the same Chevy Equinox I'd bought used back in 2007, and it was on its last leg...er, wheel. The air conditioning had gone out, the sunroof was stuck permanently ajar, and only two of the power windows still worked, but this is what I would be driving to the awards show.

Or so I thought.

I didn't grow up in a family where material things were considered a priority, so I'd never really cared about the fact that my car was a piece of crap until I had to drive it to an event where I'd be surrounded by the biggest celebrities on the planet. I was in over my head and I knew it.

The night before the show, after I'd miraculously pulled everything together, I went to wash my car. It was so banged up that I'm not sure what I thought a car wash would do, but I wasn't exactly sure if I would be parking in a lot or if I would have to drive past the celebrity entrance, or worse yet, if I would have to have a valet park it. I was trying to muster up pride in any way that I could, and washing my car was a small way to do that. There was one minor problem: the broken sunroof.

So I drove through an automatic car wash that sort of ended up being an unwanted shower, and not only was I now wet, I was also humiliated. This doesn't happen to people who walk red carpets, so it must be yet another sign that I was in over my head. Actual celebrities don't even wash their own cars, and here I was getting washed WITH mine. It was awful, and it got worse.

I exited the carwash and pulled over to the side of the parking lot, turned off my car, and broke down. I felt like such an idiot because I'd been too broke to fix the sunroof (and still was). I had no right thinking I was worthy of going to such a prestigious event and just knew that this was God's way of punishing me for actually believing for a moment that I deserved more. I felt like a fraud and I felt like a fool.

Eventually, I was able to do what I'd been taught to do since childhood: I pulled myself together and pressed forward. In the grand scheme of things, this was certainly not a rock bottom moment, although it was certainly a humbling one. I convinced myself that this was just another test, wiped away my tears, and decided to push through this roadblock, just as I had so many other times in my life. There was a problem, though: my car wouldn't start.

That was that last straw! I lost it. This time I couldn't stop crying. Every ounce of self-doubt I'd ever experienced in my life came rushing back, and I was paralyzed. I had no money in my bank account to pay for an Uber, my credit cards were maxed out, and my old-ass car was well beyond its warranty, and now I had no way to get to the Golden Globes the very next day. I'd invested everything into my dream and was closer than I'd ever been, but it was all falling apart. I was crushed.

I'd just left my cousin Lyndi's house around the corner, where I had shared how proud I was of this opportunity I'd been given, and she gladly would've picked me up and taken me home, but that same pride kept me from reaching out to her for help. She scolded me for it later, because she's awesome like that. It felt as if the universe was conspiring against me to keep me from the life I'd always dreamed of. I was not worthy.

Luckily, I'd paid my AAA renewal, so I had my car towed to the shop and reached out to my boyfriend Emile. He picked me up, both my physical body and my broken soul, and gave me a ride home, where he reminded me how deeply I am loved by so many and that this was just another test. He gave me the confidence I needed to push forward at a time when all I wanted to do was retreat and hide from the world.

The next day, I had the opportunity to interview Sandra Bullock, Chris Hemsworth, Lupita N'yongo, and Jennifer Lawrence, all because I was able to push through my fears—and the *Entertainment Tonight* credential around my neck helped, too. I would not have made it to that opportunity, one that changed my career and my life, had I not allowed myself to be loved at a time when I felt anything but worthy.

I clearly knew how to play it cool...sorry Jennifer.

Friends and family reached out to tell me how proud they were, and my social media was on fire. No one other than my boyfriend and my mom, of course, knew what it actually took just for me to make it to my very first red carpet. Back then, I was too afraid to show the world my brokenness, but it has only been through that brokenness that I've been able to find my true self, and I'm going to be honest with you: I'm kind of a fan of the guy I discovered.

I'm not a celebrity, my life isn't flashy, and by no means do I consider myself lucky, but I have chosen to surround myself with supportive people who have believed in me even when I didn't believe in myself, and I work really, really hard. It's because of those people and my work ethic that I am now able to share my heart so easily, hoping that maybe I'll inspire someone else to do the same. We're all fighting for happiness every day of our lives, some harder than others, and the only way to get there is to lift each other up every chance we get.

So if you're comparing yourself to someone you've been watching from afar, STOP. You have no idea what's really going on behind the scenes. For every moment of pure joy you see on someone's Instagram, I promise you that person has countless moments that they'd never dare share with the world. That's okay. That's human. All you can do is focus on your own journey and know that you are right where you're meant to be.

There are lessons in every experience, but it's those rock bottom moments that really show us who we are, what we want, and how far we're willing to push ourselves to achieve happiness. I found clarity in that moment and in so many moments since for which I am so grateful at this stage in my life. I live a life of profound purpose that is in no way affected by the lives of those around me. So the next time you catch yourself scrolling through social media to see the awesome things other people are up to, stop and check in with yourself. It's important to begin acknowledging unhealthy patterns so that we can do something about them. Every time you start feeling a little sorry for yourself, stop and say out loud, "I'm awesome, and I am exactly where I am supposed to be!"

On that day four years ago, the universe shut my car down to make sure I was completely alone and not distracted. Maybe it was the only way my dense brain could receive the message that I was in fact worthy, capable, and ready for the opportunity. I was…I was, and I WAS!

Against all odds, I'd made it onto my very first red carpet! It wouldn't be my last.

Script Rewrites

We live in a world where it's easier than ever to compare ourselves to others. Social media can be a wonderful thing in moderation, but having constant access to the very best moments of those we follow isn't always a good thing. It's important to keep ourselves in check and create healthy boundaries around our social media habits.

I've found that creating "sacred space" during the first thirty minutes and the last thirty minutes of my day has done wonders for my mental health. In the past, I would wake up and immediately grab my phone, scroll through my social media feeds, and without realizing it, start my day by comparing myself to those I follow. If I were waking up at 9 a.m. and someone I follow had posted that annoying type of 6 a.m. post about how they're attacking their day and achieving their goals, I would immediately feel behind. Similarly, if I scrolled through Instagram or Facebook before bed, I'd often fall asleep feeling as if I hadn't accomplished enough that day. Neither habit was intentional or healthy, so I made a change.

Now, I have a rule that the first half hour and the last half hour of my day are sacred to me. So, I am not allowed to reach for my phone AT ALL during those two windows of time. Instead, I use those spaces to set my intentions for the day before me or show gratitude for the day I've just experienced. This practice has transformed my life and made me a happier and more well-balanced human being. The act of comparing ourselves to others never leads to anything good, so try making this simple adjustment and see how it enhances your life. Also, I promise you'll sleep better at night, which is always a good thing.

CHAPTER SIXTEEN:

DISILLUSIONED AF

Scene 51: Vegas, Baby!

INT. PANDA EXPRESS — NIGHT

The fluorescent lighting of the small restaurant casts a harsh glow on the party of two beneath it, AJ, with his boyfriend EMILE sitting just opposite of him.

The RING of a bell echoes throughout the room as the cashier sends off another customer with their food.

AJ stares, downcast, into his orange chicken and fried rice while Emile chomps down, content with his meal.

AJ picks up his chopsticks to poke his food around.

Emile looks up from his own food to AJ.

"How did I get here, Emile?"

"Well, we drove here."

"That's not what I meant and you know it. I mean, how did I get to this place in my life? I'm thirty-two years old, unemployed, and so broke that we're sharing Panda Express because I can't afford to order my own $7 meal. I'm such a loser!"

Once again, I was in the midst of a rock bottom moment and Emile was there to help me through it.

"AJ, you are not a loser, so I never want to hear you say that again. You've hit a rough patch, and we're in Vegas so that you can show God you're willing to get out of your comfort zone and take work in order to dig yourself out of this hole."

He was right. I'd recently lost my job, and a buddy of mine had set me up with some interviews at a few nightclubs in Las Vegas. I was dead broke and needed to make some serious money fast!

I'd failed in Los Angeles, so what made me think I could make it in Sin City?

The answer: not much.

Los Angeles is a difficult city to survive in. The rent is expensive, the people are always focused on themselves, and the rest of the world has a tendency to look at Angelenos with a collective eye roll. I get it, we are a city of artists. People move here from all over the world to chase dreams of one day becoming the next George Clooney or Angelina Jolie. Most creative types have heard on more than one occasion, "You should move to LA; you're so talented."

There is definitely truth to the idea that a city like LA is a great place for all sorts of artists, musicians, etc. The entertainment industry as a whole is a beautiful community of progressive thinkers who are passionate in a way I'd never experienced before moving there. That passion is intoxicating. I love being surrounded by a diverse cross-section of humanity everywhere I go.

I remember my first week in LA like it was yesterday. I had signed up for a one-week actor's boot camp, and I knew in my heart that THIS would be my fresh start; THIS would be my introduction into the entertainment industry. The boot camp was filled with actors from around the world, all taking a leap of faith in a city and on an industry that would not exist without such fearless individuals. I'd decided to rebrand myself as Aaron Jason and take Hollywood by storm!

I spent $1,000 on a weeklong acting boot camp even though I had no job, nor any idea how I was going to pay the second month's rent at my new apartment with my sister Kari, but I was taking a leap of faith, dammit! I'd always been a charmer, and I figured this boot camp would be the perfect opportunity to charm my way into some TV show or blockbuster film. The boot camp was being taught by a series of acting coaches, and at the end, there would be a workshop in front of some of Hollywood's most sought-after casting directors. This was my chance to shine!

Except it wasn't. I learned very quickly that acting is so much more than smiling, saying something witty, and bullshitting your way through a scene. Acting requires remembering stuff; stuff like words and blocking and more words. Now, I'm great with words; I use them all the time. What I'm not great with, as I learned during my first week in LA, is learning other people's words and pretending like I care about them. Simply put, I bombed the entire boot camp. I went into my first week in LA with all the confidence in the world. I left with a deflated ego and no money in my bank account. Apparently, putting all my eggs in one basket wasn't the most foolproof strategy.

So, I decided to do what I did best at the time: I went to the pool. One of the great things about living in LA is that it's always sort of summer, and our apartment complex, although nothing special by Hollywood standards, felt like a resort to this small-town Ohio boy whose soul had just been crushed. It was there that I met a guy who would change the course of my life and set up the next decade of my journey. It began with him hitting on me, telling me I had a great ass, and asking if I was single. I thanked him for the compliment and told him it was complicated, and we instantly became friends.

TJ was his name, and he's one of those rare people you come across in life who just has a way with people. He had made a name for himself as the lead backup dancer for Britney Spears in the early years of her career. They had been best friends until they had some sort of falling-out, and after that, he never danced for her again. (I never asked what happened.) This small-town boy was kind of blown away to know a guy who'd traveled the world with the biggest pop star on the planet, and the fact that he was living in the same apartment complex in North Hollywood as I, lounging next to the same pool…that was just too much to wrap my brain around.

I was young.

We got to talking, and he asked what I did for a living. I explained that my plan to take over Hollywood hadn't quite gone as expected, and he offered to get me a job as a bartender at this place called the Saddle Ranch Chop House. I'd never heard of it, and I'd also never tended bar, so I obviously thought this was the perfect opportunity to get back on my feet! He introduced me to his boss Ryan, who hired me on the spot—Ryan was also who I would end up dating for the next four years. I became a great bartender, and although it wasn't what I'd moved to LA to pursue, it paid the bills and brought some really interesting people into my life.

The tricky thing about being able to pay your bills is that it can be a double-edged sword. On the one hand, I wasn't dead broke any longer and could afford to do things like eat and pay my rent, which were both great things. On the other hand, I was staying up late, drinking too much, and allowing my creative side to die a slow, painful death. My sister and I didn't move to LA so I could become a bartender, but that is exactly what I was for the next five years. The acting dream soon died, and my passion for life disappeared with it. I wasn't happy with my life, but I wasn't sure how to switch things up or how to dig myself out of this creative rut, so a bartender I remained.

I bounced around a lot, working in different restaurants, bars, and nightclubs during that period, and although I was making money, I was not fulfilled creatively or spiritually. One day, after working for a year or two at this awful nightclub called Infusion Lounge up at Universal Studios City Walk, my former coworker was promoted to bar manager. His attitude toward me started to shift; I was not comfortable with where things were going, and I let him know it. Long story short, he made up some excuse about my sales numbers not hitting goals and used that as a reason to fire me. He did it over the phone, and he tried telling me that he was doing it for my own good so that I could pursue my dreams of becoming a television host.

At this point in my journey, I had just begun taking hosting classes and honing my craft at an online network founded by Maria Menounos and Keven Undergaro called AfterBuzz TV. He knew that I was pursuing my dreams but not getting paid for that work, and he tried to use that as justification for firing me.

I told him to fuck off and sent him my sales numbers for the past year to let him know that I had them and that they were in fact higher than his, then I went on my merry way. I have a tendency to try to get in the last word whenever I can… It's something I've been working on.

Also, I probably could've used some healthier language, but I was young and angry. I don't talk like that anymore.

Well, I don't talk like that VERY OFTEN anymore.

Angry and unemployed, I had no idea how I was going to dig myself out of this situation. On the one hand, my ex-manager was right. I had moved to Los Angeles with a dream and for a purpose, neither of which were being fulfilled by me slinging AMFs to a bunch of drunk kids in their twenties at a lame club outside a theme park. I was working next to Universal Studios amidst all sorts of Hollywood history, but I was a bartender, and that was not okay with me. Also, if you're not sure what an AMF is, Google it and consider yourself lucky.

By this point, I was in the early stages of my relationship with Emile, but he was just as broke as I was and could not help me financially. I'd borrowed so much money from my parents over the years that asking them for help was not an option. I was thirty-two years old, and I was a broken man once again. I decided that it was time for a change. I decided that in order to put myself back together again, Vegas was the answer!

Yeah, THAT Vegas. I know what you're thinking, but at the time it seemed like the most brilliant, well-thought-out plan I'd ever concocted (keeping in mind my past track record of brilliant ideas, which included spending every penny on a weeklong acting boot camp that I was sure would make me the next Tom Cruise). I was going to live in LA and commute four hours to Las Vegas every single weekend for the entire six-month summer season, and I would make so much money that all my troubles would disappear. I'd heard stories of bartenders making $100,000 or more in just six months, and I was willing to travel for the opportunity to turn my life around. I had five years of bartending experience in LA, a lot of connections in Vegas, and a winning personality. It was a no-brainer!

There was one minor problem: I was dead broke.

At the time I had about $3 to my name and not enough gas in my tank to get me out of the Valley, let alone all the way to Las Vegas. There have been moments in my life where I've felt so embarrassed by my own failures that I did not believe I deserved to be alive, like I wasn't worthy of taking up space on this earth because I was such a monumental loser. This was one of those moments. I was a grown man who couldn't afford the gas money it would take just to get to Las Vegas.

I talked to my mom, letting her know how bad things were for me, but refused to ask her for a penny. She still offered, but I assured her I would figure it out like I always do and went on with my day. In the past, I have had a tendency to drop bombs on my mom like that and then act like everything's fine.

"Hey mom, I haven't eaten in a couple of days, I don't have a job, and I'm pretty sure I'm going to be evicted, but don't worry about me, I'M GREAT...I've got this!"

Sorry, Kathy.

At the time, I was probably either too insecure or too self-involved to realize the burden I was placing on my poor mom every time I'd hit her up with one of those calls, but it was the only way I knew how to unload some of my burden and give myself space to breathe again. She was also the only person besides Emile with whom I felt comfortable truly opening up. My mom knew how broken I was, even when the rest of the world around me thought everything was fine.

A few days went by, and I still hadn't been able to scrounge up any money for my day of scheduled interviews in Las Vegas. I was committed to showing up, I just had no idea how I was going to make that happen. Then, I got a note in the mail from my Uncle Tom, and with it, a check for $150.

I started to cry.

He'd talked to my mom and wanted me to know that I wasn't alone and that the entire family believed in me. He didn't want me to throw in the towel or miss an opportunity. Accepting love from anyone other than my mom and my grandmother has always difficult for me. If I had the money to give, I'd gladly help those around me 100 percent of the time, but I was having a hard time accepting this gift. I felt like such a failure at the time that I didn't want his hard-earned money going to waste on a guy who would probably just fail at this as well. I called him to say thank you; he told me there was no need to say thanks and wished me luck on my interviews.

I was back in the game.

The same friend who had set me up with the interviews got Emile and me a free place to stay for a couple of nights in Henderson, Nevada, just outside of Vegas. The money from my uncle would cover round-trip gas money, but not much more.

Luckily, we'd grown accustomed to "not much more."

I spent two days going on interview after interview, nailing each one and getting invited back for follow-up interviews everywhere I went. I was so confident in my abilities that I was already focusing on the difficult decisions I was certain lay ahead. Which club would be my top choice? How would I politely decline the other job offers? What debt would I pay off first with all this income? I felt confident and just knew this was my opportunity to turn my life around. Emile was by my side at this lowest point, but I would make it up to him as soon as the cash started rolling in. It was his first time in Sin City, and even though I felt embarrassed that I couldn't give him the experience he deserved, it's still one of his favorite trips of those we've ever taken. For those two days, it was us versus the world.

That $150 was just enough to get us there and back safely and put a little bit of food in our bellies. We returned to Los Angeles with nothing, but the trip had bonded us in a way he hadn't experienced up until that point in our relationship. But somehow, I ended up not getting a single job offer, and my financial struggles were far from over, which sent me into another period of depression as I hit rock bottom yet again.

I felt that I'd wasted my Uncle Tom's money and again proven to the world that I was worthy of nothing. That wasn't an easy pill to swallow. How could I not get hired at a single one of the nightclubs where I'd interviewed? Was I not even good enough for that anymore?

I began to unravel.

What I hadn't considered at the time but see so very clearly now is that our trip to Vegas was a pivotal moment in my life, just not in the way I had expected. Looking back, I see what was actually happening. God was slamming the door on a chapter of my life that I should've walked away from on my own years before, but had been too afraid to leave behind. The moment I was fired from the nightclub outside Universal Studios should've been a clear message to me, but like I've said before, it usually takes me a few bounces on the pavement to really understand I've hit rock bottom.

The universe was ready for me to move in a different direction, even though I was still trying to hold onto the small version of myself I'd grown comfortable playing. When things seem to be falling apart, it's so important that we take a step back and try to view situations from a different perspective. I was being pushed toward a higher purpose and was being shown love by my partner, my uncle, and my mom (who had called my uncle to let him know that I was struggling, by the way), yet all I could focus on was the fact that I wasn't getting hired for any of these jobs for which I was more than qualified.

That wasn't the lesson.

I was too focused on what I'd always known to even see the new path that was being created for me, a path that would lead me to the beautiful, exciting, fulfilling life that I am so fortunate to live now. Sometimes all it takes to find happiness is for us to get out of our own way. That trip to Vegas was, at the time, one of the most embarrassing trips of my life, but in hindsight, it was a major turning point.

Thanks, Uncle Tom. I'll pay you back that $150 the next time I see you.

Script Rewrites

If you keep coming up to the same roadblock in your life and you can't seem to break through it, consider that your path does not lie on the other side of this particular roadblock. Maybe you're being pointed in another direction. You'll only ever know the answer if you're willing to try something new. We each tend to think we have all the answers, even when our lives aren't going in the right direction. How willing are you to try charting a new course?

CHAPTER SEVENTEEN:

ENOUGH AF

Scene 82: I am Enough

INT. BREW NATION COFFEE SHOP — DAY

A fire CRACKLES in a fireplace as a WAITRESS crosses in front of it.

She makes her way to the couch where AJ is sitting reading a book and drops a coffee onto the table in front of him. She offers a quick smile then walks off.

AJ leans in to take the coffee, his eyes never straying from the book in his grasp. He takes a sip of coffee and returns the mug to the table.

He crosses one leg over the other as he turns a page, leaning back into the plush couch.

I had just spent the day finishing this incredible book by a man named Kute Blackson, and once again, it was exactly what I needed to read at exactly the time I needed to read it. Do you ever feel that way? It's so funny how God shows up for us when we need Him most. I'll admit, I'd prefer that good things happen faster and more often in my life, but this day in particular was a reminder that things always happen exactly when they are supposed to.

I like to get ahead of myself; I'm always eager to learn the next lesson before I've passed all the tests life is currently throwing my way. I've never been the most patient person, and when things get difficult or uncomfortable, I've had a tendency to throw in the towel way too soon. I really don't even know what to write about at the moment, because my first full day home on this writing sabbatical didn't quite go as planned. My bedroom last night was freezing, so

I woke up with a sore throat and an earache, then the house was freezing all day. And my mom convinced me to do a ten-day juice cleanse while I'm home, which totally sucks because I was so excited about the constant gas and trips to the bathroom that accompany the good ole hometown diet. Seriously, I shat four times yesterday! Also, eight minutes after finishing my first juice of the day, I downed a row of saltine crackers out of my mom's line of sight, God bless her soul.

I had received disappointing news about this gig in Dubai that I'd been praying for but which didn't pan out, and I would've felt upset about that, but at the moment I received the news, I had just read in Kute's book that we are exactly where we're supposed to be at all times in all ways, and in the book, he'd just told a story of a friend who said, "That's good news" no matter what the news was. So, that's good news![1]

As badly as I wanted to quit, to just throw in the towel on this crazy book writing idea of mine, I hung in there and actually did get great news to finish out the day. My taxes had just been completed, and they were WAY better than the year before. No $16,631 tax bill this time! Suck it, Uncle Sam!

I considered all of these victories, some big and some small, to be monumental successes considering where I had been just a year prior. It's important to put life in perspective from time to time. I had not only halted the negative momentum that had been building over the course of my entire life, which was a massive accomplishment by itself, but I'd managed to start building in a positive direction toward the life I desire. Yeah, things weren't going quite like I'd planned, but there was movement, and I was learning along the way. I share all of these stories because there is a common thread, and it's one I'm sure many of you can relate to in

---

1   Kute Blackson. *You Are the One: A Bold Adventure in Finding Purpose, Discovering the Real You, and Loving Fully*. Gallery Books, 2016.

your own lives. My expectations were not being met, so I was getting frustrated. Damn you, universe, you've won again…or have you?

Expectations are a momentum killer in so many ways. The textbook definition of the word expectation is "a strong belief that something will happen or will be the case in the future." Also, and I really like this definition, "a belief that someone WILL OR SHOULD achieve something." Expectations can be powerful motivators, but they can also be the source of deep depression. We are both blessed and cursed by the ability to visualize how certain periods of our lives will pan out, and even though we all know things rarely play out in real life the way they do in our minds, we still set expectations. The problem is when those expectations aren't met, we're left frustrated and wondering what we did wrong.

I had expected to churn out 2,500 words per day and finish my sixteen-day writing sabbatical with half of my manuscript complete, but when I failed to hit that goal on day one, then again on day two, and again the following day, I felt like a complete failure and was embarrassed that I'd ever believed I was capable of doing something as huge as writing a book. Once that doubt started to creep in, it gained momentum and became my new truth. I was in over my head.

I remember graduating high school with a solid ten-year plan in place. I would go to The University of Toledo on a four-year track scholarship, graduate at age twenty-two, move to New York City, and begin my career as an actor, which would prepare me to make the leap to late-night television. After five years or so of booking acting gigs, I'd be asked to take over *The Late Show with David Letterman*, since he'd surely be ready to retire by then. It would be a difficult decision for him, but one made easier after seeing the immense talent of this newcomer from Celina, Ohio. I would carry on his legacy, and CBS would be my home for the remainder of my long television career.

Now, you may be wondering why I would choose a network like CBS back in 2003, at a time when NBC was dominating the television landscape. Well, the answer is simple. I thought Letterman was a badass, and I preferred the idea of living in New York versus LA, which is where *The Tonight Show with Jay Leno* was being filmed at the time. Not even the world's gayest logo, NBC's rainbow peacock, could keep me from my dreams of thriving in The Big Apple!

Needless to say, my ten-year plan was a total bust. It seemed so logical at the time, but it was never actually a plan. It was more of a fantasy that I had no idea how to make into reality. My expectations were not met, and David Letterman held onto his job until 2015; the dude had WAY more stamina than I'd predicted! My expectations for myself fell flat, and I wasn't sure how to move forward. I'd come to the end of those ten years and felt like a complete failure. That's not a good feeling.

Each time I failed to achieve a goal or came up short in life, I fell deeper and deeper into depression. These weren't even expectations being placed on me by anyone other than myself, but they felt heavy, and I felt like a loser. I allowed myself to start doubting my potential more and believing in my achievements less, which is never a healthy combination. Once that Pandora's box has been opened, life starts rolling downhill quickly, and before you know it, the smallest everyday task begins to feel like a measure of your entire life. Something as simple as your frustration that the latte you ordered at breakfast wasn't quite hot enough turns into a laundry list of the things you hate about others, about your life, and eventually about yourself. This creates a victim mentality and allows each of us to justify giving up on our dreams, because the alternative just seems too difficult. The alternative can be wonderful, but we have to have a plan that is capable of helping us achieve the expectations we place on ourselves.

So let's first figure out how to set healthy expectations. Most people, myself included, go through much of life not even realizing what it is that's frustrating them. More often than not, it's unmet expectations. I just read an article recently about a study on this very topic that listed unmet expectations as the number one cause for divorce.[2] Not money, not cheating…UNMET EXPECTATIONS. That blew my mind at first, but it started to make more sense once I allowed myself to consider what it actually meant.

From the day we're all born, expectations are placed on us by our parents, by other family members, and by society in general. These expectations aren't necessarily a bad thing in theory, but they snowball as we grow older and begin to navigate life on our own. The crazy part is that while these expectations are placed on us, expectations we never asked for, we also begin to expect things of ourselves and of others.

Remember all those absurd expectations I'd placed on my unborn children when I was in junior high? Yeah, it's been a pattern in my life, and I'm willing to bet it's a pattern that has popped up in your life from time to time as well.

Now, let me be clear: Some expectations are necessary in life, or we'd all be jobless wanderers committed to nothing and no one. I'm not about that life. Also, I've technically been jobless since being let go from *Hollywood Today Live* over two years ago and have been without steady income for most of my life, so no judgment. I freelance enough to pay my bills, and I've decided to focus on this book for the next year, because my personal story has been in need of some serious rewrites! If I were sitting on my couch watching talk shows all day and striving for nothing, I'd feel like a loser.

---

2   Olivia Petter, "Biggest Threat to Marriages Revealed by Relationships Expert." *Independent*. October 24, 2017. https://www.independent.co.uk/life-style/love-sex/marriages-biggest-threat-revealed-relationships-expert-unmet-expectations-a8016976.html

I know, because I've done that! Sometimes I prefer *The View* and sometimes I prefer *The Talk*, but I ALWAYS love me some Wendy Williams! Her show is all kinds of messy and I love it!

Luckily, I've always been able to pick myself up eventually. You're only truly failing when you decide to do nothing about life's rock bottom moments, and I know it's sometimes easier said than done not to go that way, but it's crucial if you want to live the life of your dreams. The trick is becoming aware of as many expectations as possible in order to have the capacity to weed through the good and the bad, deciding which to accept as healthy and which to toss to the curb. Here are a few guidelines that might help you navigate that process.

First, are your expectations fair?

You can never expect more of the world or of anyone in particular than you are willing to give. The only way to fulfillment is through giving.

Do you expect to come home to a clean house with a hot meal on the table prepared by your partner while he or she struggles to get through their own day in their own way, raising your children and washing your dirty drawers at the same time? If you're upset every time you come home and realize that your partner is not, in fact, a superhero, well, that's on you. It's why the world feels extra special during the holidays and why we feel so complete after helping out a loved one in need. As long as you're always giving at minimum 51 percent in every relationship that you have, you're doing your part. Now, not all relationships will be worthy of you, and there will come times when you have to make difficult decisions about who or what you will allow in your life, but for every relationship that you cherish, always aim to give at least 51 percent. You'll know how much you care about someone based on how much effort you put in. It's also a good way to measure how much someone cares about you. If you're not getting what you're giving and are seeing that as a pattern, it's time to move on to people and relationships that fulfill you. It's scary, but necessary.

Next, at what point in your life did you develop these expectations, and do they still make sense in your current situation?

This one will take some deep introspection and probably some therapy if you really want to get a clear answer. Now, I'm not a therapist, but I've been to a few, and I highly recommend them (except for that one who recommended my ex and I try out a threesome; that didn't quite turn out the way I'd hoped). Overall, therapy is a wonderful tool for helping us navigate all sorts of emotions, and it doesn't necessarily have to come from a licensed therapist. Also, if your therapist tells you that a threesome might be the way to save your relationship, FIND A NEW THERAPIST!

I'm not saying that you should or shouldn't go to a therapist, but what I am saying is that I realize it's not a reality for some people financially, and until it becomes feasible, there are other options. Most of my own "therapy" has come from trusted family and friends. I'm pretty much an open book, at least according to what most people probably think, but when it comes to the real stuff, I play it close to the vest. If you casually know me, you might think I'm living the dream, interviewing the biggest names in Hollywood, traveling the world and attending the dopest events. Sometimes, all of those things are true. Sometimes. The reality is that most of my life has been a struggle, and the very small number of people who know the depths of that struggle are the people I really open up to. Those people are my everyday "therapists." It takes time to figure out who those people are, but the more you start asking yourself some tough questions about who you are, who you want to be, and how you plan on getting there, the clearer it will become who your true friends are.

So let's say you've decided on a path to your own personal happiness and surrounded yourself with the most supportive people you can find. This is a great start, but your best-laid plans will all fall apart if you do this one thing that I'm sure you do, because every human being in the history of humanity has done or is currently doing this. Are you ready? This is really important, and I need you to pay very close attention, because the secret I'm about to tell you is some of the most profound, life-altering bit of advice you'll ever receive. It seems simple, but is actually quite difficult.

NEVER COMPARE YOURSELF TO ANYONE ELSE!

Seriously, never do it! You may be thinking that I just tricked you, that I just gave you some crap advice that you've heard a million times over in your life, advice so obvious that even the worst parent has given it to their children too many times to count. But what I challenge you to examine is whether or not you've actually, genuinely, at your core taken this advice to heart and put it into action in your day-to-day life.

My guess is you haven't. If you had, you wouldn't be holding this book right now, because you either wouldn't have picked it up in the first place or you would've tossed it aside in disgust after the big reveal just a few sentences back. Since you're still with me, I'll assume that you feel just as messed up as the rest of us, so I'll continue. Also, we are ALL messed up, so welcome to the club, and stop beating yourself up for that one.

When we make comparisons, whether we realize it or not, we're really just telling ourselves that we don't stack up, that we're not as good as some other person, or that we don't deserve the things that we're comparing.

I'll share an example.

During my first month of hosting classes, back when I met Kristen Brockman, I also met a guy named Justin Walter. He was kind, charming, and very talented, and he scared the shit out of me! I remember the first time we were given copy (which is what a script is called in the hosting world) and asked to present it to the class. There were maybe a dozen of us in that class, and we were each given five or ten minutes to review the copy before getting up in front of the room.

One of the reasons the whole acting thing never worked out for me was that I am TERRIBLE at memorizing things. I'm not talking about information, because that's something I'm actually quite gifted at memorizing. Words written by another person that I'm expected to say as my own; THAT has always been difficult for me. Apparently, though, Justin didn't have the same struggle.

He volunteered to go first, which the rest of us were fine with, because we were all desperately trying to memorize our lines right up until the last possible moment, or at least I was. The copy was a solid three to four paragraphs long, so we weren't expected to have it memorized, but our teacher Maureen wanted us to present it as naturally as possible.

Homeboy struts to the front of class and leaves his copy at his seat!

WTF?

He was ready to rock and roll; I was still trying to get the first paragraph down!

"Is he really going to do this thing from memory?" I asked Kristen.

"Maybe he's really good at memorizing things, I don't know."

We watched in awe as he nailed the entire thing without missing a beat. I was both impressed and defeated. How on earth had he just done that so effortlessly? When it was my turn to go up, I held onto my copy for dear life, made all kinds of mistakes, and returned to my seat feeling like a complete failure. All of the positive momentum I'd built in the classes leading up to that moment had been erased, and I was left wondering yet again if I was in over my head. I had compared myself to Justin and felt as though I didn't measure up.

So, I quit taking classes. For the next few months I stewed and I spiraled. I thought I'd finally found my thing, but how could I expect to be the next David Letterman if I couldn't even outshine Justin Walter in a hosting class on a Wednesday night in Culver City?

What I should have been asking myself was this:

How can I learn to memorize copy as well as Justin?

OR

Why do I quit things whenever they get difficult?

OR

How can I learn from this experience and use it to become a better host?

At first, I did none of those things. I avoided all of the icky feelings that accompany those sorts of tough questions. Eventually, I picked myself up and got back in the saddle, so to speak, but I could've avoided all of that time I wasted in between if I'd just done one simple thing differently. If I hadn't compared myself to someone else, someone with a different skill set and a different destiny than me, I never would've lost the momentum I'd built and found myself scraping the pavement again, lost in doubting myself.

I bounced back and it all worked out. Now, I rarely compare myself to anyone, and this has given me the freedom to explore my desires, to express myself freely, and to make mistakes and learn from them. Maybe if I'd never met Justin, I wouldn't have learned that lesson. I'm glad I did, though, because he pushed me to be a better version of myself, and at the end of the day, that's all any of us can do.

Like Kute said in his book, "We are exactly where we're supposed to be at all times in all ways."

Had I not been THERE, I might never have found my way HERE. Here I know that I am talented, I am capable, I am resilient, and I AM ENOUGH.

Script Rewrites

For this exercise, I'm going to send you to my website at www.AJGIBSONTV.com. There you'll find a great printable FREEBIE to help you shift your self-talk narrative. Follow the simple instructions and start creating some new, healthy habits today!

CHAPTER EIGHTEEN:

STILL BROKE AF

Scene 94: Tapped Out

INT. AJ'S APARTMENT — LIVING ROOM — NIGHT

The DRIP of a faucet can be heard over the
hush of a quiet room.

AJ's long fingers wrap through his dark
brown hair, pulling painfully at the scalp,
as he sits down on the couch. His elbows
plant themselves firmly on his knees as he
lowers his head down between them and toward
the floor.

He takes in long, deep breaths, a few of them
catching in his throat.

Emile stands before him, arms crossed and
worry plain in his eyes.

"AJ, you've got this. I know this process has been difficult for
you, but you have to keep writing. You need to see this thing through
to the end, and the world needs to hear what you have to say."

"That's sweet, Emile, and I appreciate what you're trying to do
right now, but I am in debt up to my eyeballs, I don't have a job, no
one is hiring me, and I have $10.14 in my bank account!"

I'd been writing this book for months, and money was tight. I
hadn't earned a paycheck in a while, and I was scared.

"Boo, I know how scared you are right now, but I also know
that God is using you. Think of every person who has ever struggled
with all of the same issues you've dealt with your entire life and
how much this book will help them. If you give up now, you'll never
know what you could've accomplished. You need to take your own

advice and dig deep. I know this book will change people's lives, and I know it will change yours, but you've got to finish it!"

I was feeling vulnerable and drained, unsure of myself and unable to see past my current fear-based mindset. My boyfriend was using my own advice against me. At first, it pissed me off, but then it motivated me. He's really good at doing both of those things.

Full transparency, I'm feeling really insecure right now. I've pushed through so many personal roadblocks to get to this point in the book, and yet I still feel like a fraud. I feel like I'm not notable enough to write a book and that I'm not worthy of giving advice that I don't always take myself. These fears are real, but they are not based in reality.

I WILL finish this book, because I NEED to finish this book. I am unwilling to accept this false narrative that I'm nothing more than a bullshitter who never sees things through to the end, so I'm sticking with this thing. If you're still here with me, THANK YOU.

CHAPTER NINETEEN:

FOCUSED AF

Scene 99: A Tethered Life

INT. ANDAZ HOTEL - CONFERENCE ROOM - NIGHT

The large yet swanky room is packed with a majority of WOMEN and some MEN seated in rows of chairs positioned at the front of a stage.

On the stage sits AJ atop a high chair looking out over the vast audience, their gaze planted firmly on him. Their pencils occupy their notebooks, lead at the ready.

He adjusts his posture as a bright smile crosses his lips; an air of confidence surrounds him.

To his side is ERIKA, the moderator, holding a microphone to her lips.

"AJ, what sort of advice would you give to young people who are interested in doing what you do—to those looking to carve out their own path in entertainment or as entrepreneurs?"

"That's a great question, Erika, and I always talk about the importance of being tethered to something greater than yourself. For me, I know that God put me on this planet in order to connect with people, not only to inspire others to chase their dreams and find their purpose, but to remind them to have some fun along the way. The journey should be fun, but when it's not, when the winds of self-doubt or the winds of fear start to blow you off course, as long as you're tethered to a greater goal, you'll be fine."

"I love that, AJ. What is it that you're tethered to?"

This question is my favorite, because I've spent a lifetime figuring out the answer. Also, I was being asked it in front of a room full of powerful women who were eager to hear my response. The moderator, my dear friend Erika De La Cruz, had invited me to speak at her "Passion To Paycheck" event, and I did not want to let her down.

"I do everything that I do because I love people. When the road gets difficult, I remind myself of that young LGBTQ teenager who is struggling to survive high school because he or she feels alone and unseen. I think of all those adults who hold prejudice in their hearts simply because it's all they've ever known and how important it is that I reach them to have a conversation that will hopefully spread compassion. I make the choices I make so that I give myself opportunities to impact positive change in people's lives, so when my journey gets difficult, I think about everyone who's waiting on me to help them along their own journey, because I believe that many of those people will then turn around and help the next person out. And that's the only way we create the type of world we all want to live in."

I love being interviewed because it gives me a rare opportunity to speak freely. As a TV host, my words are rarely my own. Sure, I can say what I want, but as an interviewer it is my job to make the other person shine. When I'm being interviewed, I get to let it fly!

This idea of "the journey" is so daunting to most people, but it is a concept that has been written about since the beginning of time. I believe that it's so daunting because as humans, we all desire to be in complete control of our lives. Spoiler alert: that's simply not realistic or even possible. In order to take away some of the anxiety of the unknown parts of the journey that lie ahead, I often speak not only about the importance of tethering yourself to an end goal, but also of breaking down the journey into small, workable chunks. Trying to get from A to Z is an overwhelming concept, but simply getting from A to B is something we do every day. So by creating healthy patterns aimed at bringing us closer to the thing to which we are all tethered, we can build the momentum necessary to carry us all the way to Z.

Here's another way to describe this concept.

I'd like to explore the idea of only holding ourselves accountable for what is immediately in front of us and nothing more. It's real easy to set lofty goals, to get all pumped up about the potential in our dreams and then go nowhere because we're not exactly sure how we're going to get to the place we yearn for so desperately. Maybe your dream is to be President of the United States (because apparently nowadays anyone can do that), or maybe you want to walk the runways of Paris and Milan, or maybe you want to become a police officer, but you're not sure how to make your dream happen, so you allow uncertainty to slowly creep into that space previously filled by your hopes and dreams. Uncertainty is a dream killer, but it's manageable, and sometimes the best way to deal with it is by getting in your car and driving...sort of.

To illustrate this idea, I often share the story of my sister Kari and I moving from New York to Los Angeles, and I focus in on the importance of headlights. If you're driving your car at night, headlights become crucial not only to you reaching your destination, but also to your getting there safely. Whether you're on a cross-country trip at night or trying to get through a long day at work, it's never a good idea to focus on anything other than what is directly in front of you at any given point in time.

Let's head cross-country in our minds for just a moment.

Say you know that your goal is to make it from New York to LA, but it's dark, so you turn on your headlights and begin your journey. Now, those headlights do not reveal LA to you immediately, that would be crazy, but what they do reveal to you is the road immediately in front of your vehicle, so that's all you need to focus on at the moment. Once you can accept that, amazing things will start to happen.

As you drive and reach the end of the path being revealed by your headlights, the next bit of your journey will be revealed. As long as you keep doing your part and continue to move, your headlights will do their part and continue to reveal more of the road ahead. To me, headlights are a perfect analogy for how God works in our lives.

If we don't show up, He doesn't show up.

Now, the road will not be easy and the path won't be straight, but as long as you keep moving, you will arrive at your destination at exactly the moment you were intended to get there. There are thousands of routes that could get you to LA, and you'll take a few "wrong" turns along the way, but as long as you stay focused on your end goal, you WILL get there.

There is a graphic that I came across once on Instagram that perfectly illustrates the difference between what we think success looks like and what it actually looks like. You will make unexpected turns, roads will be closed, and you might need to stop to rest from time to time, but if you are tethered to a goal greater than yourself, you will arrive.

I can feel this book coming together, and there are not words to express how deeply grateful I am to you for reading my words. I've fought hard for this moment, and the journey has taken me thirty-seven years, but every moment of it has been worth it. My headlights are beginning to reveal my purpose, and let me tell you, that's a profound sight to behold.

Script Rewrites

What do your headlights reveal? What is one goal that you'd like to work toward starting right now? For me, using a tool called a "Focus Wheel" has really helped me to find clarity on my goals and create the space to achieve those goals. This simple but effective tool was created by Abraham-Hicks, a non-physical form of intelligence interpreted by a woman named Esther Hicks. I know how strange that sounds, but trust me, this thing works!

Google "focus wheel" and print one out for yourself right now. In the center circle, write out "I love…" and then complete that statement by writing something that you want to manifest in your life; make this a big goal. After doing so, in each section surrounding the center circle, write the words "I love…" again, and then complete each statement with words that support the statement at the center of your wheel.

At multiple points throughout your day, read this entire wheel out loud to yourself and feel the words begin to manifest. Say them out loud, look into a mirror, and FEEL the power of the words you're speaking. Do this until you've achieved your center goal, and when that happens, write a new wheel. I cannot overstate how helpful this simple tool has been in my life. It's time to get focused!

CHAPTER TWENTY:

MEANINGFUL AF

Scene 102: Time's Up at the 75th Golden Globes

EXT. BEVERLY HILTON HOTEL — RED CARPET — DAY

Hands carefully adjust a dashing black bow tie. The same hands lower to straighten a "Time's Up" pin along the chest beneath the bow tie.

We CUT DOWN to shoes that shine under the Red Carpet lights.

We PAN UP to see AJ dressed in a dashing black velvet tuxedo, surrounded by equally well-dressed CELEBRITIES.

AJ puts a hand on his earpiece to listen.

PRODUCER (V.O.)

We're on in 5...4...3...2...

AJ smiles as he puts the microphone to his lips.

"Coming to you LIVE from The Beverly Hilton, I'm your host AJ Gibson, here today with my partner in crime, you love her five days a week on *The Real*, Miss Jeannie Mai!"

"Awww AJ, we love you too, and I'm so excited to be here with you again this year! It's going to be a great show."

"That's right, Jeannie. Tonight we're going to be talking to some of the biggest celebrities on the planet, and it all starts now. Welcome to the 2018 Globes Red Carpet LIVE!"

And we were off to the races! For the second year in a row, Jeannie and I were at the heart of Hollywood's biggest party, but this year would be more than just a party. Not only was this the seventy-fifth anniversary of the Golden Globes, bringing the worlds of television and film together like no other awards show, it was also at the center of a global social movement.

The Time's Up movement had taken the entertainment industry by storm, and the Golden Globes red carpet would be its international coming-out party.

I'd been asked to join the show a few weeks prior by the team at Dick Clark Productions, with whom I'd worked for years, covering the American Music Awards, the Academy of Country Music Awards, and the Billboard Music Awards in addition to the Globes. I watched every single nominated film, binge-watched as many of the nominated shows as possible, and picked out the perfect tux!

In my early years, finding red carpet looks to fit my 6'5" frame was not an easy task, especially working without a stylist and on a very tight budget. Celebs like Jeannie get dressed by designers; I was not a celeb like Jeannie. However, I had recently begun working with a British menswear line called Suit Supply, and they had agreed to dress me for the Globes. Not only do they have dope suits and tuxedos, but many of them come in LONG! If you're oddly shaped like me, then you understand how it feels to find clothes that fit your body type. I picked out the perfect tux and went to my fitting, and the alterations were done...on my navy blue tux.

Any other year that wouldn't have been a problem, but if you've followed the Time's Up movement at all, then you're aware that it used the red carpet at the Golden Globes to make a statement. To support the countless women who had been bullied, sexually harassed, or even assaulted, every major celebrity walking the red carpet would be wearing BLACK!

Aaaaaaaahhhhhhh! I'd finally gotten to a place in my career where a designer was willing to dress me for a major event, and it had to be the one time I couldn't wear color? Keep in mind that this decision had been settled on just days before the event, so I was left scrambling. Luckily, the team at Suitsupply was able to pull out an all-black look for me and get it tailored in time. I was NOT going to be the asshole who looked like he didn't support women, no matter how fly I looked in that blue tux!

I'm so grateful they hustled so hard for me, because literally everyone showed up in black that day. The team at Dick Clark had gotten their hands on only one Time's Up pin—which they gave to me. I was deeply honored, especially when I was told after the show that Ryan Seacrest hadn't even been able to get his hands on a pin, which felt like a small victory to me. I had something that even one of my idols didn't have!

More importantly, I was standing in solidarity with women and a movement that would change the world. THAT mattered to me deeply.

That day solidified so many things for me. For the first time in my career, I was able to have the types of conversations I'd always wanted desperately to be having with people who have the ability to influence societal norms. Shailene Woodley brought Calina Lawrence, an indigenous woman and activist from Washington state, to our stage with her, where Calina shared statistics on missing and murdered indigenous woman and those fighting to bring them justice. My heart ached as I saw the pride not only in Calina's eyes as she shared stories of her people, but in Shailene as I watched her stand proudly by Calina's side, knowing the importance of these stories. I was playing a small part in sharing an important narrative, and the gravity of the opportunity was not lost on me.

As we spoke with Debra Messing, or Grace Adler as I'll always think of her, I could see the passion in her eyes and hear the power in her voice.

"We're here to say this is it! Change is coming; change is here. We are done with discrimination, and we need diversity, and intersectional gender parity, and equal pay! We're here to support and thank all of the whistleblowers who came out and made this whole movement possible."

WOW!

These incredible women who I'd admired from afar were now standing inches from me and speaking truth into the world in a way that sent chills down my spine. For the first time, I fully understood the power of this kind of influence and saw firsthand that when given the opportunity, the celebrity machine can be used as a powerful vessel to catalyze change. I'd seen it time and time again from afar, but being there at the center of it inspired me to keep pushing and reassured me that I can in fact blend my career in television with my desire to cause positive change and improve the lives of others.

Suddenly, so many of the fears I'd had began to slip away. This movement and the strong women behind it inspired me to embrace my true self as well. I may have been wearing a borrowed tuxedo, and my bank account may have been empty, but my life had purpose that day, and I knew I didn't want that feeling to disappear.

So I pressed forward. Time was up on slimy men in positions of power taking advantage of those seeking to be seen and heard and respected as equals. I was raised by strong women and taught to always respect others, but why was it so difficult for me to see myself the way I've always seen others?

After the show, I felt different. I felt like I'd just been a part of history, and I was proud of the work I'd done, whether or not anyone else had noticed. Our show was watched by over five million people that day, so I knew the conversations that had taken place would have a positive impact on someone, somewhere.

Jeannie and I were exhausted, but so very proud of the work we'd done.

Later that night, my executive producer Rika pulled me aside and told me it was my best red carpet performance yet. Just as she had the night of that crazy awards show at the El Capitan Theatre, Rika answered my prayers. God has a funny way of using others to speak to us, and her words assured me that I was on the right path and that I was worthy of the moment.

Script Rewrites

Sometimes it's the strength and courage of others that inspires us to give that last push! Journal about someone whose strength inspires you and why. There are no wrong answers here.

You can write about a family member, a friend, or someone you read about online. Write about this person; write about what they did and why you think they are so special. What do you admire about this person? How would you like to be more like this person? What one thing can you do today that will make the world around you a better place, and that you think would cause that person to be proud of you?

Get writing, and then go out into the world and be awesome...the world needs you. Who knows, maybe someone else will end up writing a journal entry about YOU!

CHAPTER TWENTY-ONE:

PURPOSEFUL AF

Scene 117: Daytime Emmys & Real Life Tragedy!

INT. AJ'S APARTMENT — HALLWAY — EVENING

AJ and Emile make their way down the hallway toward their apartment. They tow their luggage behind them, the wheels of their bags clicking against the tiles of the floor.

As they turn the corner to approach their front door, they are confronted with a blue sticker sealing up the neighboring door.

AJ leans in closer to read the sticker.

It's from the coroner's office.

AJ's eyes widen.

"Emile, why is our neighbor's door sealed with a notice from the coroner's office?"

"Ummm, I'm not sure. Let's get inside, and then I'll call the phone number on the sticker."

My heart sank, and I felt the sudden urge to vomit.

Two days prior, I'd presented at The Daytime Emmys. Miss Vivica A. Fox and I handed the award for Outstanding Morning Program to the team from *Good Morning America*. It was one of the coolest experiences and proudest moments of my career, and they had even aired part of the clip the next morning on *GMA*... That was awesome! I always love when people reach out to tell me they just saw me on TV; the support means the world to me. I've worked so hard to get opportunities like this one, and I felt an unexpected sense of comfort on that stage in front of a theater full of so many of my colleagues, many of whom are also personal idols of mine. That was the universe telling me that I belonged…that I was again worthy of the moment.

Presenting at the Daytime Emmys alongside the FLAWLESS Vivica A. Fox was a career highlight. I will forever be grateful to my mentor and friend David Michaels, senior vice president of the Daytime Emmys, for the incredible opportunity. Photo Cred: Bill Dow

I enjoyed the accomplishment for about forty-eight hours.

My boyfriend Emile and I spent the day after the Emmys poolside in Palm Springs. We work really hard and decided to give ourselves this single day to relax and put career goals to the side. It's so important to check in with ourselves from time to time, and if you're in a relationship, as I am, it's also important that your partner knows you're still engaged and present. We enjoyed the mini vacation, but the next day we headed back to LA and the grind continued.

As Emile called the number on the sticker, my mind started to spiral. I'd just spoken to this neighbor, Robert, two days before while I greeted my makeup artist and my date for the Emmys.

We'd decided to get ready at my place and leave from there. Robert had spent the morning standing in the doorway and mumbling to himself. I'd seen similar unnerving behavior from him before; we'd been neighbors for seven years.

It left my guests and me feeling uncomfortable both for him and for ourselves, so I made the decision to call security. I'd never done this in the seven years that we lived just inches from each other.

"Hi, my name is AJ, and I'm not sure what can even be done, but my neighbor has been standing in his doorway rocking back and forth all morning and mumbling to himself. He's done this before, but I have guests, and it's really freaking them out, and it's freaking me out now too. I'm not sure if you can send someone to check on him, but I would hate if I didn't call and he ended up doing something to himself or to someone else."

"Sir, we completely understand, and we'll send patrol over to check on him shortly."

I thanked the man on the other end of the phone, and we continued to get ready for my big day.

As we left for the Emmys, we kindly wished him a good afternoon and headed for the tenth floor elevator. It was the last time I'd ever see him.

As we were entering the elevator, three security officers were exiting. I pointed toward our neighbor's apartment and mouthed, "Please, just make sure he's okay," and then we were on our way.

As I paced back and forth in our living room recalling the events of the past forty-eight hours and beginning to take ownership of this devastating event, Emile got some information from the number he'd called. Robert had jumped from his living room window the day before while Emile and I were sipping margaritas poolside in Palm Springs.

I immediately collapsed on the couch. How was this possible? Why would he make such a tragic choice? What could I have done to prevent this? Was there anything I could've done to show him more kindness in the past seven years? I had called security on him for the first time in seven years, and hours later, he had taken his own life. Was I to blame for this man's suicide?

My mind was going to some pretty dark places..

I was taking full ownership of this monumentally tragic decision that our neighbor had made. I knew it wasn't rational, but I'd never experienced something quite like this, and the swell of emotions consumed me. The wall between our apartments and the space between our front doors was no more than eight inches or so wide. Eight inches away this man had struggled, alone, for seven years, in an apartment that is an exact replica of ours, only flipped. We'd witnessed odd behavior from him before but had never considered that this could happen. How could someone ever make that choice? I asked myself over and over, "Could I have helped this lost soul?"

I prided myself on living authentically and connecting with others, yet I'd failed for seven years to connect with a man living just inches away. That's been a tough pill to swallow, and the emotions keep hitting me at the most random times. I feel guilty for not doing more, grateful that I was not home to witness his death, and fearful of what could've happened had he made a different choice and decided to act out in a different way, possibly harming myself or someone I love.

Mental illness is so often overlooked because the stigma attached to it tends to make us uncomfortable. I'm not sure if he'd ever been diagnosed, but it's clear to me that he was not well and unfortunately saw only one way out. That breaks my heart.

My family came to town the following week, and that helped me to cope. Emile's mom was here, too, and she prayed for me, which eased my heart immensely, but the weeks afterwards were difficult. Finding a way to get back to "normal" proved to be a tall order. I spend most mornings home alone, sitting at my desk and working on my book while Emile is out earning a paycheck. Usually, I love this time alone because it's my time to be creative and write from the heart. In the weeks following Robert's death, however, I wasn't able to focus because our apartment complex had finally begun the process of cleaning out his space.

In my family, when someone passes away, we all come together to reminisce and share stories of our lost loved one. Their possessions are divided up compassionately and given to whomever appreciates them the most. Robert apparently didn't have friends or family, which made his story all the more tragic. For weeks, my mornings were spent listening to random men tear apart his home and throw his life down the trash chute, about six feet from my front door. It was devastating.

I felt anxious for weeks and on the verge of tears.

Each time I left my apartment, I struggled to stay calm, and each time I returned, I would unlock my door with my head down to avoid catching a glimpse of that blue sticker, which remained on his door for nearly a month. One morning, I said a prayer and then opened my door to head out to a coffee shop, only to find a large trash bin blocking my way. It was about five feet tall, and I had to physically remove this bin filled with Robert's belongings just to exit my own home. That hit me hard.

I'm a pretty resilient dude, and I make the choice to live each day with gratitude and joy. That wasn't easy in the weeks immediately following his death.

I had suffered from depression at different stages in my life, and as I processed the emotions attached to this tragedy, I could not help but feel compassion for Robert. Less than two years prior, staring out my bathroom window—less than a foot from his window—I'd nearly made the same choice. When faced with the same decision, he'd made a different choice.

If that isn't some profound shit, I don't know what is.

I could feel that the universe was sending me a message, but I wasn't sure what it was. I was feeling some weird version of survivor's remorse, mixed with this deep guilt for having called security, layered on top of the shame I was feeling for having spent the past few months typing away at my computer, working on a book while my neighbor suffered in silence.

I later found out that security had been called multiple times both before and after I'd made my call the day of the Emmys, and that certainly eased some of my sense of guilt. The LAPD had even sent a unit to his apartment with a psychiatrist, who'd cleared him.

I KNEW at that point that his decision was not a result of my phone call, but my heart still ached for him.

One morning, as I was leaving my apartment, the young man who'd been tasked with throwing away Robert's belongings stepped onto the elevator with me, pushing a bin of my neighbor's things.

The bin was full of dress shirts still on hangers covered in plastic from the dry cleaners.

"Hey, buddy," I said, "I know this is some pretty heavy stuff, and I'm sure it's not easy, but we all appreciate the work you're doing. Just know that I'm praying for you."

This young man, maybe in his mid-twenties, looked up at me with a look that showed me how deeply he appreciated those words. "Thank you. Sometimes people just hide stuff."

Wow.

His words hit me hard, probably because they were both simple and profound at the same time. They were the sign I was looking for. Everyday people go through stuff; I do, you do, we all do!

One decision could have sent me out my window, but instead I chose to take a step back, reevaluate my life, and chart a new course. If my goal was to write a book that could change lives, I could not let his tragedy stop me from sharing my story. I realized in that moment that this is all about so much more than him, or me, or any of the roadblocks and rock bottom moments I've had to overcome to write this book. Robert saw no option other than to take his own life. If this book could help even one person fight depression and find happiness, then I would finish it not in spite of his tragedy, but because of it. I am determined to finish this book to honor him and to honor every person whose story was never shared.

The Daytime Emmys protected me from being home to witness Robert's tragic end, but his decision reminded me of the importance of connecting and sharing our common hopes, fears, and dreams. We're all in this together, so I press on.

Script Rewrites

As humans, we are designed to bring meaning to every experience. Two people can experience the very same thing and each have a very different take on what happened because of the meaning they choose to give the experience. Think of two or three of the most difficult moments in your life. Write about them, but write from the perspective that they were a catalyst for important growth and change. For example, in this chapter, experiencing a death so close to home could have sent me into depression. Instead, I chose to take it as an opportunity to do more with my life to help others.

At the start of this process, I was able to use three very traumatic situations in my life to find clarity and "flip the script" on my own life. Getting fired from *Hollywood Today Live* freed me up to accept freelance opportunities that have helped me to discover my true passion of public speaking. Feeling judged by my sister forced me to dive deeper into my relationship with God and listen to my heart. Receiving that tax bill brought me to the edge and almost took me out completely, but instead turned out to be more of a rebirth. Without these moments, I would not have gone down this path, and you would not be reading this book.

So I challenge you to dig deep and create a new narrative around the events in your own life that you may previously have considered to be negative experiences. This isn't easy, but this perspective shift has the ability to free you from your past and allow you to move into your future with freedom. Good luck.

CHAPTER TWENTY-TWO:

THANKFUL AF

Scene 120: Thanks, Rock Bottom Moments!

INT. AJ'S APARTMENT — NIGHT

AJ is lying in bed, his MacBook Pro resting on his lap. The light being emitted from the computer highlights his features against the dark background of the bedroom.

AJ CLICKS the trackpad, opening the manuscript to this book.

He grins as he realizes there is only one chapter left to write.

He is filled with deep pride.

EMILE enters the room.

"How's it coming, boo?"

"Ummm, I'm almost done."

I could not believe that I was finally speaking those words. Seven months after beginning this crazy journey, I was able to complete my manuscript and send it over to my publisher.

"So, what do you have left to write?"

"Well, that's what I'm struggling with. I know how I'm ending this book, but I feel like I need to acknowledge the journey and the people that have helped me along mine. I don't know how to do that."

I could see the wheels turning in Emile's head. He's one of the most creative people I know and always knows just what to say each time I find myself struggling to get over a roadblock.

"Well, why don't you actually write a letter?"

Hmmmm.

"You mean, write a letter to myself, or to my journey, or to my readers?"

I wasn't sure exactly where he was going with this.

"YES."

That didn't really clear things up for me.

"What do you mean, yes? I should write a letter and then do what with it? Use it as a chapter?"

"YES."

That sounded kind of crazy to me, but it also sounded exactly like something I would do. This is my book, after all, so I can write it any way I want. If writing a letter is the best way to show how grateful I am, then that's what I'll do, so here goes.

Dear Life,

We haven't had the healthiest of relationships over the years, but we have experienced every single moment of my journey together. You are the only thing on this planet that knows exactly who I am, what I've been through, what I believe, why I feel the way that I do, and who I want to be. You have been my 'ride or die' companion since Day 1 and will be there until the day that I take my last breath. While I hope that day is many, MANY years from now, I would like to take a moment to acknowledge you and say THANK YOU for all that we've been through so far.

Thank you for blessing me with a family that has loved me through it all, regardless of disagreements or belief systems that don't align. I know that my family loves me, and that's the most important thing in the world to me.

Thank you for making my journey so difficult. I've been ready to throw in the towel a few times and came really close that night in my bathroom, but thank you for seeing enough in me to pull me back from the edge.

Thank you for giving me the opportunity to host some amazing television, but more importantly, thank you for taking opportunities away from me that were not meant for me, opportunities that I was too afraid to walk away from on my own.

Thank you for teaching me to live within my means and to budget the little that I do have so that when I am blessed with financial freedom in the future, I will be more mature and able to handle my finances properly.

Thank you for showing me that I am capable of anything I set my mind to. Writing this book has been the scariest, most frustrating thing I've ever attempted, yet here I am about to turn my manuscript in to my publisher.

Thank you for giving me the beautiful gift of my sexuality. This burden has been especially difficult to bear, but through my struggles I've developed a deep compassion and empathy for those who feel marginalized or discriminated against, and for that I am so grateful.

Thank you for Emile. He truly has been my rock through so many of my personal rock bottom moments.

Lastly, but certainly not least, THANK YOU for encouraging me through a slow but steady journey to find and develop my own personal relationship with God. This has challenged me on a level that I cannot describe, but the payoff has been so very beautiful. Please continue to stand by me as I strengthen this bond.

With Deepest Gratitude,
Me

CHAPTER TWENTY-THREE:

HAPPY AF

Scene 125: The Billboards Bounce Back!

EXT. MGM GRAND — RED CARPET — NIGHT

PRODUCER (V.O.)

And that's a wrap!

AJ smiles brilliantly as he lowers the mic from his lips, his smile as blinding as the lights surrounding him.

His co-host ERIKA JAYNE plants an approving hand on his shoulder before being ushered down the carpet.

AJ takes the earpiece from his ear and starts toward the entrance of the MGM Grand. AJ's STAGE MANAGER approaches and takes the earpiece and microphone.

Emile meets him down the red carpet with a kiss, and they walk in, hand in hand.

"Great show, boo."

Emile was by my side for another successful red carpet, but this time was different.

"So, were you nervous?" I asked in response.

Emile got a big grin on his face and nodded yes.

We'd just walked our first major red carpet together and proclaimed our love to the world. Eighteen years after I'd come out for the first time, I was doing it all over again with my boyfriend of nearly six years by my side. I had shown the world my authentic self, and it felt sooooo good!

I'm thirty-seven years old, and in some ways, I feel like I'm just now getting to know myself. For much of my life, whether I was aware of it or not, I struggled with self-love. It's always felt so natural for me to show love and compassion to others, but showing the same to myself has never been easy. I'm not a selfish person, I know that, but in some weird, messed up way, self-love has felt like a negative thing for most of my life.

One of my best friends, Dr. Therese Mascardo, once told me that she couldn't imagine me saying a fraction of the things I say and think about myself to my worst enemy on my worst day. She was right. I'm great at being the happy, fun-loving guy, but there has always been a part of me that's been tortured by negative self-talk and paralyzed by fear: fear of failure, fear of looking stupid and above all, fear of actually succeeding and then losing the people I love because they can't accept this new, happy, TRUE version of me.

This same fear has kept me "small" for many years. I dated guys that I thought I deserved instead of those who inspired me to be better and do better. I accepted unhealthy patterns with family members because I was too afraid to express how I really felt. I spent years circling the drain as a server and a bartender because I was too afraid to step out of my comfort zone and try fighting for the life of my dreams. I've been deeply hurt by many new "friends" that I thought wanted to build a relationship with me as badly as I wanted to build one with them.

The thing is, we're all flawed. I can't count how many times I've tried reaching out to someone I had just met with whom I felt a connection, only to realize they were not as interested in getting to know me as I'd thought. That's not a good feeling. So I've gotten really good at playing it close to the vest, so to speak. Not many people get close enough to know the real me, but I'm just not okay with that anymore. I want to know everyone, I want to celebrate everyone, and I want to lift up every person I meet so that they can live the life they were created to live.

It's why I decided to write this book.

But I will not sacrifice myself as a stepping-stone; those days are gone.

Instead, I'm using my voice to draw people into my life who see the same value in me as I see in them. We were all created to live connected lives, so this book is my call to the universe.

CONNECT ME WITH THE RIGHT PEOPLE TO BRING ME CLOSER TO THE LIFE I WAS CREATED TO LIVE!

As we wrapped another successful carpet, one watched by over ten million people globally, I was most proud of the moment Emile and I had created before the show. Holding his hand and kissing him in front of the cameras was something I'd always dreamed of doing but hadn't had the courage to do in the past. Writing this book has changed so much for me. Sharing my story and receiving deeply encouraging words from complete strangers on social media has given me the strength and the confidence to go deeper, to reveal more. For three years now, I've been lucky enough to land this gig, but this year, I decided to be bold.

Days before heading to Las Vegas, I told my Emile that I wanted to walk the red carpet with him. (I'm talking about the part of the carpet where the press pool lines up and photographers snap the pictures you see in tabloids and on the internet.) He'd never walked a major red carpet in his life, but I know he'll walk many, because he's a superstar in the making—and I wanted his first time to be with me. So I made up my mind that this was going to happen, and I came up with a game plan...sort of.

You see, typically, the couples who walk the red carpet and have photos taken together are famous. If not both of them, at least one of them is, so it makes sense. Well, I'm not exactly famous, and neither is Emile, but I've got people to inspire, causes to promote, and love to spread!

Representation is so important, and although we never had same-sex couples as role models to look up to when we were younger, we both know there are LGBTQ youth around the globe who DO need to see themselves reflected in the world. So, logically, I thought to myself, "Why don't we show our love on the red carpet at the Billboard Music Awards. Only MILLIONS of people will be watching. What could go wrong?"

So, I decided it was happening, and Emile was on board!

The morning of, I could tell he was nervous. I was too, but I couldn't let him know that, because I was the one who had actually been invited to walk the red carpet, so I had to keep my shit together. As I was escorted to the top of the carpet, I grabbed his hand and didn't let go. We approached the entrance, which was being run by a PR firm, with confidence. We knew that the worst thing that could happen would be that we would be told he couldn't join me for photos, which would've been fine. However, we also knew that if we did walk the carpet together, the pictures of us that would be published might bring hope to a young LGBTQ person somewhere, so the risk was worth it.

But no one questioned us, and we were BOTH escorted onto the carpet; and as the photographers started shouting, "AJ, over here…AJ, look to your left…AJ, up here please," I held Emile's hand tight, and with pride flowing from my heart, I planted a kiss on my partner's lips. The flashing lights doubled and then tripled, and now, instead of just hearing my name, I heard the photographers shouting, "Can you kiss again, please? Just one more kiss! Guys, can we get one more kiss, please?"

Emile and I on the red carpet at the 2018 Billboard Music Awards, allowing the world in. Photo Cred: Jim Ruymen/UPI

It went by in a flash, literally, and we walked back into the holding area to cool off indoors for a few minutes before my hosting duties were to begin. Emile was overwhelmed, but the only two people on the carpet who had any clue that was so were now standing in that air-conditioned room, catching their breath after the chaos of it all. It's almost like we were waiting for someone to come scold us or kick us out of the event for walking together, like someone was going to come say, "You're not famous enough. Someone, please escort these two out!"

The funny thing about fame, success, and all those weird titles, is that someone does not hand them to you; you simply decide that you belong, and guess what, YOU BELONG. We decided that we were ready not only to express our love for each other in a more impactful way, but to express our love for our LGBTQ brothers and sisters in a way that might have a positive impact on lives.

The journey I began as a child and had continued while writing this book had come to a climax. I was pulling strength from my grandmother, from my mom, from my friends, and from the women who had spoken so bravely in support of the Time's Up movement. Their courage sparked something inside of me, and I was determined to see that spark turn into a raging fire!

The weekend was intense, and the red carpet was nuts, but through it all, our love only grew deeper, and the love we have for ourselves became stronger. We'd always assumed the world knew we were together, but apparently it wasn't as clear as we'd thought. So many people had thought we were just buddies or coworkers.

Coming out is a funny thing. I'd always considered that day in my parent's living room as the day that I "came out," but in reality, I've been coming out my entire life in so many different ways. We all have. Each time we find the courage to share our dreams with the world or live in our authentic truth, we are coming out to the world. Living publicly isn't always an easy choice, but it gives us each the potential to impact so many lives.

Not only is it okay to reveal ourselves to the world, it's necessary.

At the 2018 Billboard Music Awards, I not only talked the talk, I walked the walk. I literally walked down a red carpet with my boyfriend! How cool is that?

In that moment, I decided that I would never again play small in order to make other people comfortable, and I am so grateful that Emile was the person right beside me for such a pivotal moment in my life. He'd been there through so many of my rock bottom moments that it only made sense that he be there for the moment when I decided to own my awesomeness. A part of us that religion and society had told us to hide or at least diminish for our entire lives was on full display that night, and the world has reacted in a way we weren't quite expecting…with love. If complete strangers can show me this kind of love, surely it's okay for me to love myself more deeply. And for you as well, please don't be afraid to do the same. Be authentically you, share your stories, and never be afraid to LOVE YOURSELF!

Speaking of love, when your co-host Erika Jayne is in the midst of a "lover's quarrel" with her boss, Andy Cohen…you just step back and enjoy the show!

Script Rewrites

This exercise comes from my best friend, Dr. Therese Mascardo. She's not only a licensed therapist and a woman of God, she is one of the most compassionate human beings I've ever met. During a dark period of my life, she used this technique on me; it rocked me to my core and shifted the way I talk to myself. In the last chapter, I wrote a letter to my life. Here is your chance to write a letter of your own, but we're going to take a different approach this time around.

For this rewrite, I'd like you to take a situation in which you've been hard on yourself, beating yourself up, or saying discouraging things to yourself. It sometimes really helps to write this self-talk down on paper. Perhaps you're saying things like, "I'm a failure," "No one cares about me," "I'll never get this accomplished," or worse. Now take the exact same circumstances, but instead of them being about you, imagine they are happening to your BEST FRIEND, or someone whom you care about very much. Next, write a letter to your best friend to encourage them. What would you say to that person? When they say negative things about their situation or themselves, what words would you use to encourage them and lift them up? Would you use the same words that invade your mind every time you feel like a "failure?"

Next, read the letter out loud, but this time, receive the encouragement for YOU and allow the message to resonate. Keep this letter nearby; make copies of it and keep one in your car, at your desk at work, or even taped to your bathroom mirror. If you're running out of space there, find a new place to keep a copy of this letter. Pull it out from time to time and remind yourself that YOU are just as important as your friend in the eyes of God and in the eyes of those around you, so cut yourself some slack and show yourself some kindness.

I remember the day Therese and I did this exercise while sitting in a coffee shop, and the words she said to me then will stay with me forever.

"AJ, I know your heart, and I know the type of man that you are, and I also know that on your worst day, you wouldn't talk about your worst enemy the way you talk about yourself. I think that's something we should examine and something you should pray about."

We did, I did, and that simple perspective shift changed me. I hope it does the same for you.

CHAPTER TWENTY-FOUR:

PERSPECTIVE AF

Scene 133: AJ Finds Peace

EXT. COFFEE SHOP — DAY

AJ sits alone at a table on the patio of his favorite writing location.

Cars race down the busy street as AJ's fingertips gently tap the keys of his laptop.

A grin washes over AJ's face as he realizes that he's about to finish writing his FIRST book.

When I began the process of writing this book, I had an idea of how I thought it would all play out. As I've done so often in life, I thought I knew where this journey would lead me. I could not have been more wrong.

I had no idea what I was getting myself into, and that's a good thing, because I probably would've talked myself out of this crazy idea of mine had I known how difficult it would be. I set out to rewrite my story and was sure I knew where that would lead me. Last year, when I started this journey, I was in a very dark, scary place. My life lacked purpose, and my days were without meaning. In my heart, I was hoping to bookend my story with some great news about my sister Kari and I. Never in a million years did I think we'd still be at the same place nearly three years after that conversation on the sidewalk.

We're cordial and check in on each other from time to time, but our relationship remains fractured. I wish I could tell you something different, but that's the truth. Initially, that made me feel like a complete failure. In my head, I could not finish or publish this book without having arrived at a full healing with my sister. Encouraging you to flip your own script felt inauthentic, considering the fact that I'd not been able to do that same thing with the deepest, most painful personal relationship in my own life. Again, I was wrong.

You see, this story has not ended, and although I am hurt that she still has this belief system about my life, I am no longer affected by it in the way that I was when I started down the path toward sharing my story. Writing my truth has given me a freedom I had not considered and led me to places I never thought I'd go.

Earlier this week, I spent three days in Denver, Colorado, workshopping and delivering a new talk for the very first time. In it, I shared the story of my sister and myself. In preparing to give this talk, I had to practice it in small groups and onstage multiple times. I've always wanted to develop my public speaking skills but was having a difficult time sharing such a deeply painful experience, especially in front of complete strangers. Each time I was called to run through my talk, I would begin to tear up at the mention of my sister. I was still hurting, but I knew that my story would help others going through similar painful situations, so I was encouraged to fight through the heartache.

Hours before giving my talk, I was onstage one last time, rehearsing, and when I began to talk about my situation with Kari, I began to cry again. Luckily, it was only a practice run, and the founder of the workshop, Melanie Spring, was sitting in the front row and had some helpful insight for me.

"AJ, you keep crying every time you mention that you and your sister found your way back to faith together; maybe that's something you're still working through, so let's take it out of the talk for now."

She was right. The last thing I wanted to do was get up on that stage and fall apart, but that was and is such a huge part of our story that I felt it was necessary to share it. Religion has been the single greatest roadblock of my life and the source of more pain than anything else, and my sister had used that thing to hurt me, after

I'd brought her back into the fold. We were baptized together as adults, but both of us went down very different paths from that point forward, and I don't see that changing any time soon.

I even sent her the chapter "Gay AF" from this book nearly two weeks ago in an attempt to show her that I am not writing about her in a malicious way, but in a way that tells our story from my perspective. I explained to her how badly I needed to get this story out of me because the burden of carrying it had become too great to bear. I reminded her how deeply I love her and assured her that this story is one of hope, no matter how dark it might seem at the moment. She has yet to respond.

In the past, that would've sent my brain into a tailspin of despair. I would've taken on her inability or unwillingness to engage with me as a fault of my own. I probably would've deleted the chapter and apologized for hurting her, just to keep from rocking the boat. The problem with that approach is that it would lead to the same results. I would've continued to hurt, she would've gone about her life unaware of my true feelings, and the world would be the worse for it. So, I pushed through.

"You know, Melanie, you're right. It's still a really difficult thing for me to talk about, and this talk is a huge step for me, but I know how important our story is, so I'll figure out a way to make it work without breaking down."

The event was only hours away, and I had no idea if I would be able to get through it without crying, but I knew I had to try. So as the other speakers were making their last-minute adjustments and running through their own talks, I separated myself and did the only thing I knew could help me deliver this talk in a way that would be powerful and uplifting. I prayed.

I prayed for the right words to come to my lips, I prayed that my intentions would come through in my talk, and I prayed that my sister would feel how sincerely I want to have a healthy, loving relationship with her. She wasn't there watching my talk, but many of my family members were watching it via livestream, so I knew that Kari might see it at some point, and I wanted my words to be heartfelt.

The talk went better than I could've expected. I received a warm ovation, and as I walked off the stage to the back of the room, I felt the gravity of the moment hit me. I'd just shared with complete strangers the story of that day on the sidewalk when my sister, in an attempt to love me, ripped my heart out, I'd talked about being fired from what had once been my dream job, and I'd revealed that I'd almost taken my own life over a tax bill. It was a terrifying experience, but it was exhilarating in ways I hadn't expected. I walked off that stage feeling like a new man.

Sharing the darkest parts of my story in front of a room full of strangers for the first time was terrifying AND liberating! Photo Cred: Mary Gardella

As I reached a private space, outside the view of the audience, I broke down. I'd cried a lot over the course of the past couple of years, but these tears were not the same as those others. These tears represented a freedom, a sense of pride, and a new beginning. For the first time since those three events took me to my rock bottom moment and nearly out that tenth-story window, I felt like me again. I'd survived the worst period of my life and come out the other end better for it.

I'd set out to rewrite my story, but I learned along the way that God was sending me down this path to actually FIND my story.

Every time we try to dictate outcomes or stick to the plan we think we're supposed to stick to, we create roadblocks and lose sight of life's true purpose. We were all created with purpose and for a purpose, but sometimes we need really crappy things to happen to us to set us on a new course. I am so grateful to have been fired from *Hollywood Today Live* and for being called "all icing and no cake," because without the sting of that moment, I might never have had the desire to show the world what I'm capable of. Had my sister never used her faith to judge me, I might never have leaned harder into mine and become aware of God's purpose for my life. And if I hadn't received a tax bill for $16,631, I might never have realized the limitless value of my own soul. Every single one of those rock bottom moments knocked me down, but I've realized that rock bottom really can be a beautiful place. When we're at our very lowest, if we're open to it, there is a peace that comes with ultimate failure and in that peace we have a rare opportunity to listen, to learn and to grow.

I've grown into the man I always dreamed of being, but I could not have done so without first being stripped of everything. On that cool October night back in 2016, as I held onto the sides of my open bathroom window, staring at the pavement ten floors below and picturing the end, I was given the gift of a new beginning. In that moment, I was too ashamed to look up, fearful that maybe I *was* actually all icing and no cake, fearful that my sister was right and God really did want me to change, and fearful that maybe my soul actually wasn't worth more than $16,631. Today, I know my worth.

My life has purpose, and I am content fulfilling that purpose on my own, because I know that no matter what, I am never truly alone. I was divinely created for a very specific purpose, and my job is not to give away my power to the voices of those who might not understand me, but to give power to those whose voices are not heard and understood.

CONCLUSION AF

I've got great news for you, you are now into a new "scene" of your life. This does not mean that your past scenes are set in stone or that they won't come back into play as you move forward. You can always revisit your past to see what lessons remain to be learned. Apply those lessons to the person you continue growing into— because your script can always be rewritten.

The journey is not always easy, but that's a great thing if you allow the process of your journey to build you into the person you were truly created to be. This book is not a guideline aimed at helping you find your specific purpose, but it can be a source of inspiration as you venture out into the world and discover the person you were born to be. My hope is that you don't have to hit rock bottom as often as I have to figure that out, but if you do, I hope you come back to this book any time you need to be reminded that you are capable of change, that you are uniquely made, and that you are loved. Each and every one of us has a story to tell, but the human experience is not linear, and it's not always easy. Remember that as you move through life discovering new things about yourself and about the world around you.

Also, if there is still breath in your lungs, you still have time to flip your script. So, what are you waiting for? I believe in you, the world needs to hear your story, and YOU deserve to live the life you were created to live. It's time to say goodbye to the pavement and set your sights on the sky, because it's your time to soar!

For me, the adventure has just begun. Less than eight months ago, I decided to write a book. In just a few moments, I'll be turning my full manuscript in to my publisher. I also dreamed of becoming a successful public speaker, and I've made that dream come true as well. I was at an all-time low less than a year ago, yet I've been able to turn it all around, and I've accomplished many of my dreams in such a short amount of time. I've learned that I'm capable of so much more than I'd previously thought and that I have the power to make any dream come true, as long as I'm willing to get uncomfortable and put in the work. Instead of pretending to have all the answers, I've grown accustomed to taking on a student mentality, and that simple shift in perspective has opened me up to a whole new world of possibilities.

Now, as I wrap up this project, I am filled with excitement as I consider the endless possibilities for my life. I believe that this book has the potential to be a bestseller and change the world, but if only one person buys it and it positively impacts that one soul, I've done my part. I know that I have the ability to become one of the all-time great public speakers, but if my words save the life of just one person seeking connection, then I am okay with that. I am confident that the love I have for others will continue to lift me up as I go out into the world with a renewed excitement for life and a deep sense of purpose.

I am no longer afraid of sharing my story, and I have found unbreakable strength in the vulnerability that comes with this new version of myself. I am more confident than ever, I am more passionate, I am more humble, and most importantly, I am more grateful than the guy who sat down to tell his story eight months ago.

I am grateful for my struggles, I am grateful for my victories, I am grateful for the lessons life has taught me, and I am grateful to be alive. The truth is that YOU are the thing that pulled me back from the open window that night and YOU are my purpose in life. God always works through us in ways we often never see, but I see very clearly how He used each of you to save me. My love and deep compassion for all of you kept me from stepping out that window and helped me step into the life of my dreams. I am forever indebted to each and every one of you and will do my best to make you all proud. At the same time, I know that I cannot change the world alone, so I am calling on YOU, the person reading this book right now, to get out of your comfort zone, flip your script, and share your story with the world. You might not think the world needs to hear what you have to say, but I promise you this...your story is more powerful than you know.

Rock bottom is a gift. In this place where we are stripped of everything, we are given the gift of freedom: freedom to start over, freedom to let go of the personal roadblocks holding us back, and freedom to reach out and grab the life we were created to live!

Acknowledgments

As you may have realized, I haven't always believed in myself or in my ability to write this book, so I'd like to take a moment to thank the people who've stood by me through my rock bottom moments and always offered a helping hand.

First and foremost, I need to thank the big guy upstairs. My faith journey has been long and winding, but without the love of Jesus Christ, I would not be here and you would not be reading this. At the same time, I know how difficult faith is for so many and I also know how awful humans can be, especially when using their faith to hurt others. Let me apologize for their behavior on His behalf...that does not represent Him.

I'd also like to thank my mom for being the perfect mom for me. I could not imagine getting through a day without you and hope I don't have to know that feeling for many, many years. Grandma is dead, but you're very much alive and for that I am deeply grateful.

To my sister Mackenzie Kuhn, you are an incredible young woman and I am so grateful for your help on this book. Not only did you design the silhouette on the cover, but you wrote the intro to EVERY chapter and did so beautifully. You are now a published illustrator and author at the age of twenty-two...not bad! LYBMS ;-)

I also need to thank my sister Kari for loving me. We may not be on the same page too often these days, but I know we are both on journeys that will one day bring our relationship to a place of healing. Being your big brother has been the greatest honor of my life and I know how deeply you care for me, so please know the feeling is absolutely mutual. I will love you with all of my heart from now until infinity.

To my sister Chris, you are a superhero and the greatest role model I could've ever asked for. I am in constant awe of you. To my Pops, Mr. Steven Laverne Kuhn, you are one of the coolest people that I know, you have the patience of a saint, and your support since I was a young boy has helped mold me into the man that I am today. And to the rest of my family, thank you for raising me with love, laughter, and kindness.

To my dad, I know your life hasn't been easy and I know you never meant to hurt me. I see the man you have become, I appreciate the effort you've made to know the man that I've become, I love you, and I am so grateful to call you my father.

To my friends, Therese Mascardo, Elena Schelich, Susan Williams, Kennelia Stradwick, Erika De La Cruz, Sofia Stanley and Nadia Stanley…you have all lifted my spirits more times than I could ever count, and I am eternally grateful. My journey would not be the same without each of you by my side.

To my mentors, Maureen Browne, Karen Donaldson, Steve Holzer, Josh Kaplan, Oliver Talamayan, Hank Fortener, Alain Torres, Ben C Allen, and Melanie Spring, thank you for seeing me when I couldn't see myself, for setting a positive example in all that you do, for always encouraging me use my voice for good, and for pushing me to step out of my comfort zone.

To Krissy Lindquist, Rika Camizianos, Alexi Mazareas, and the rest of my Dick Clark Productions family, thank you for making me shine, for supporting me and for giving me opportunities at a point in my career when I wasn't sure I'd ever work again. Words could never adequately express my gratitude.

Lastly, I'd like to give a very special thank you to the love of my life, Emile Ennis Jr. You have sustained me during my darkest days and believed in me during my many, many "rock bottom" moments. I owe you my life. I could not imagine going on this journey with anyone else and I can't wait to see what the future holds for us! No one has ever understood my heart quite like you, and I am so excited for more people to know your heart as well. Our LGBTQ brothers and sisters need our love, and your deep faith has inspired me to fight to share every bit of love I have to give. I love you…pretty a lotta bit!